The Gol

and other plays

Steve Fitzpatrick

$\not{t}00$

The right of the
University of Cambridge
to print and sell
all manner of books
was granted by
Henry VIII in 1534.
The University has printed
and published continuously
since 1584.

Cambridge University Press

Cambridge

London   New York   New Rochelle

Melbourne   Sydney

Published by the Press Syndicate of the University of Cambridge
The Pitt Building, Trumpington Street, Cambridge CB1 1RP
32 East 57th Street, New York, NY 10022, USA
10 Stamford Street, Oakleigh, Melbourne 3166, Australia

First published 1985
Reprinted 1986

Printed in Great Britain by
David Green Printers Ltd, Kettering, Northamptonshire

British Library cataloguing in publication data

Fitzpatrick, Steve
The Gold of Lies, and other plays-(Dramaworld)
I. Title   II. Series
822'.914   PR6056.18

ISBN 0 521 27893 7

GR

Performance
These plays are protected by copyright. For permission to give a
public performance of any of the plays where an admission charge is
made, please write to Permissions Department, Cambridge
University Press, The Edinburgh Building, Shaftesbury Road,
Cambridge CB2 2RU.

Contents

STAGE DIRECTIONS

There are two kinds of direction in this playscript. Those in **bold type** provide information that is essential to an understanding of what is happening in the play at that time. For a play-reading, these should be read by a separate reader.

Those in *italic type* are less essential stage directions and offer suggestions to assist with a production of the play on stage. In a reading they are best not read out as they will hamper the flow of the play, although those who are reading may find that some of these instructions offer help with the interpretation of their lines.

The Gold of Lies

CHARACTERS

STRANGER	2ND HOUSEWIFE
MAID-SERVANT	KING
INN-KEEPER	LORD CHANCELLOR
INN-KEEPER'S WIFE	CAPTAIN OF GUARDS
THIEF	QUEEN
MERCHANT	PRINCE
MERCHANT'S WIFE	COURTIERS (of both sexes)
1ST HOUSEWIFE	GUARDS

Scene 1

In front of an inn. There is a bench or something similar somewhere on stage.

(Enter Stranger, carrying a lump of gold.)

STRANGER — *(To audience)* I am a traveller. After a long journey across the mountains I've arrived here in a country no one has ever visited before. Who knows what strange people and customs I may come across? I must be careful. But fortune has been kind to me. I found this lump of gold in the mountains, and when you've got gold you can always get anything else you want. But since I've never been here before I can't trust anyone. Who knows what villains and liars I might meet?

(Enter Maid-servant, carrying bottles of beer which she puts down on the bench.)

MAID-SERVANT — Hello. What's that you've got there?

STRANGER — *(To audience)* She's seen my gold! – *(He hides the gold. To Maid-servant)* Nothing. Nothing at all.

MAID-SERVANT — Nothing? That's strange. I could have sworn I saw you holding something.

STRANGER	Well, yes, I was. It's gold. But I don't want anyone to know about it.
MAID-SERVANT	Gold?
STRANGER	Yes. *(He shows it to her.)* See? I found it in the mountains. But don't tell anyone I've got it.
MAID-SERVANT	But suppose they ask me?
STRANGER	Say you haven't seen anything.
MAID-SERVANT	But I did see it.
STRANGER	Yes, I know. But pretend you didn't. Tell a lie.
MAID-SERVANT	Tell a lie? What's that?
STRANGER	Eh?
MAID-SERVANT	I've never heard of telling a lie before.
STRANGER	You've never heard of telling a lie?
MAID-SERVANT	No.
STRANGER	*(To audience)* Hmn. The girl's obviously a half-wit. *- (To Maid-servant)* It's perfectly simple. When you say something that isn't true it's called telling a lie.
MAID-SERVANT	I thought it was called making a mistake.
STRANGER	No, it's making a mistake if you do it without meaning to. If you do it deliberately it's called telling a lie.
MAID-SERVANT	Deliberately making a mistake? But what's the point of that?
STRANGER	*(To audience)* I've never met anyone so stupid. I really think she doesn't know what telling a lie is. Either that or she's a very clever liar indeed. *- (To Maid-servant)* Never mind. It doesn't matter. Are you the maid-servant at this inn here?

MAID-SERVANT   That's right.

STRANGER   Where's the inn-keeper? I want a room for the night.

MAID-SERVANT   He's busy at the moment. He's having an argument with his wife.

(Enter Inn-keeper and his Wife, arguing.)

INN-KEEPER   No, no, no! How many times do I have to tell you?

INN-KEEPER'S WIFE   All I want is a new dress –

INN-KEEPER   You had a new dress seven years ago! What's wrong with that one?

INN-KEEPER'S WIFE   It isn't new any more.

INN-KEEPER   Well, you're not having another one and that's final. I want a new coat. That's much more important. – *(Noticing Stranger)* Who's this?

MAID-SERVANT   It's a stranger. He's been explaining to me about telling a lie.

INN-KEEPER   Telling a lie? What's that?

STRANGER   *(To audience)* Him as well?

INN-KEEPER'S WIFE   I've never heard of telling a lie before.

STRANGER   Never mind. It's not important. – Are you the inn-keeper here?

INN-KEEPER   That's right.

STRANGER   I'd like a room for the night.

INN-KEEPER   Certainly.

STRANGER   I hope your locks are strong. I'm very worried about thieves.

INN-KEEPER Oh, there's no need to bother about that. If I see a thief I'll come and warn you.

STRANGER Well, that's very kind, but how will you know if he's a thief or not?

INN-KEEPER I'll ask him.

STRANGER But if he's a thief he's hardly likely to tell you, is he?

INN-KEEPER They always do.

(Enter Thief.)

Here comes somebody now. - Excuse me, are you a thief?

THIEF Yes, I am actually.

INN-KEEPER *(To Stranger)* There you are, you see. - *(To Thief)* What are you doing around here?

THIEF I've come to try and steal some of your beer.

INN-KEEPER Oh, yes? And how do you think you're going to do that?

THIEF I was going to wait until you weren't looking.

INN-KEEPER'S WIFE That's clever.

INN-KEEPER Yes, I hadn't thought of that.

STRANGER *(To audience)* They're mad, all of them!

INN-KEEPER We'll have to make sure we keep an eye on it. - *(To Stranger)* Now then, what was it you wanted? A room for the night?

STRANGER That's right. How much will it cost?

INN-KEEPER Well, let me see now... What have you got?

STRANGER I'll pay you in gold.

INN-KEEPER   Gold?

STRANGER   That's right.

INN-KEEPER   What's gold?

INN-KEEPER'S WIFE   I've never heard of gold before.

STRANGER   What's the matter with you people? Haven't you heard of anything?

(Meanwhile the Thief has stolen some bottles of beer while the Inn-keeper and his Wife weren't paying attention. The Inn-keeper now notices.)

INN-KEEPER   Wait a minute! Where's my beer gone?

INN-KEEPER'S WIFE   Someone must have stolen it.

INN-KEEPER   *(To Thief)* Here, you! Did you steal my beer?

THIEF   Yes, I did. I told you I was going to.

INN-KEEPER   Give it back!

THIEF   All right. *(He gives back the beer.)*

INN-KEEPER   And take that! *(He hits him.)*

THIEF   Ow!

INN-KEEPER   We'd better put this inside where it's safe. - *(To his Wife and Maid-servant)* Come along. - *(To Stranger)* Excuse me a moment.

STRANGER   Of course.

(The Inn-keeper and his Wife and the Maid-servant go off with the beer.)

THIEF   Ah, well... You win some, you lose some...

STRANGER   You're the worst thief I've ever seen in my life.

THIEF   Really? Most people think I'm rather good.

STRANGER   You're terrible! How do you expect to get away with it if you always tell people when you steal something?

THIEF   But he asked me. What else could I have done?

STRANGER   Hasn't anyone in this country ever heard of telling a lie?

THIEF   Telling a lie?

STRANGER   This is incredible! I've travelled all over the world. I've been to countries where the people eat each other, where they're so primitive that they've never discovered the wheel, and never learnt how to cook food. But never, in all my travels, have I come across people who didn't know how to lie.

THIEF   But how *do* you lie?

STRANGER   Listen. The next time you steal something, if someone asks if it was you, say no.

THIEF   But that wouldn't be true.

STRANGER   Exactly. It's called telling a lie. It's very useful. Whenever someone wants to get himself out of trouble, or impress his friends, or cheat his enemies he tells a lie. It never fails.

THIEF   Let me get this straight. I steal something, but I say that I haven't.

STRANGER   That's right.

THIEF   You know, you might be on to something there.

STRANGER   At last!

THIEF   That's very clever. It's just what I need in my line of work. Did you think that up all by yourself?

(Enter Inn-keeper.)

INN-KEEPER   *(To Thief)* Right. I've hidden that beer where you'll never find it.

THIEF	Where have you put it?
INN-KEEPER	In the cupboard under the stairs. - *(To Stranger)* Now then. You wanted a room, you said?
STRANGER	That's right.
INN-KEEPER	So we've just got to settle how you're going to pay for it.
STRANGER	As I've said, I'll pay in gold.
INN-KEEPER	I don't know what gold is. Have you got any cabbages?
STRANGER	Cabbages?
INN-KEEPER	Rooms cost ten cabbages a night. Mind you, we've got rather a lot of cabbages at the moment. You haven't got a chicken, by any chance? You can stay two nights for a chicken.
STRANGER	You don't know what gold is? What do you use for money?
INN-KEEPER	Money?
STRANGER	Yes, money! How do you pay for things?
INN-KEEPER	Well, as I was saying, if you haven't got any cabbages or chickens, I'll accept eggs, fish, saucepans-
STRANGER	But I've only got gold.
INN-KEEPER	Oh. - Well, what is gold anyway?
STRANGER	*(Showing them his gold)* Look. I'll show you. This is gold. See? **(He puts it down on the bench.)**
INN-KEEPER	*(Looking at it)* Never seen anything like that before.
THIEF	*(Also looking at it)* It seems to be some sort of yellow metal.
INN-KEEPER	Most peculiar. I don't think I want any of that, thank you.

THIEF	No, nor me.
STRANGER	Don't want it? It's gold!
INN-KEEPER	Yes, so you said. But what use is it? What can you do with it?
STRANGER	What can you do with it? You can do anything with gold!
THIEF	Can you eat it?
STRANGER	Well, no, you can't eat it. But it's the most valuable thing in the world. Everybody wants gold.
INN-KEEPER	Why?
STRANGER	Because it's so valuable. No matter what you might want you can get it if you've got gold.
THIEF	How?
STRANGER	You give it to people in exchange for things.
INN-KEEPER	Things?
THIEF	What, like cabbages and chickens and things?
STRANGER	Anything you like.
INN-KEEPER	It seems an unnecessarily complicated way of going about it. Who are these people who want gold so much?
STRANGER	Everybody I've ever met apart from you. – Just take my word for it. People will do anything to get gold. They kill and cheat and scheme and grind their neighbours' faces in the dirt. They tell lies –
INN-KEEPER	Tell lies?
THIEF	Do people ever steal it?
STRANGER	They're always stealing it!
THIEF	*(Thoughtfully)* Really...?

STRANGER	Gold is the most wonderful thing in the world. Rich misers gloat over it, beautiful women adorn themselves with it, great empires are built with it, labourers work for it, beggars beg for it, thieves steal it – everybody wants gold!
	(During this speech the Thief sneaks up to the gold and steals it.)
INN-KEEPER	No. I'm sorry. No cabbages, no room.
STRANGER	This is ridiculous! *(He notices the gold has gone.)* My gold! It's gone! Someone's stolen it!
INN-KEEPER	It was probably the thief.
STRANGER	*(To Thief)* Here, you! You stole my gold, didn't you?
THIEF	Me?
STRANGER	Yes, you!
THIEF	*(After a deep breath. Loudly and distinctly)* No. I didn't.
STRANGER	What?
THIEF	I didn't steal your gold.
STRANGER	That's a lie!
THIEF	That's right. Don't you remember? You're the one who taught me how to do it.
STRANGER	Give me my gold back!
INN-KEEPER	But he says he hasn't got it.
STRANGER	He's lying.
INN-KEEPER	Lying?
STRANGER	Look, gold doesn't just disappear.
INN-KEEPER	Doesn't it? I told you – I don't know anything about gold. If it's as wonderful as you say why shouldn't it be able to disappear?

STRANGER He stole it! – I'll make him give it back.

(He advances threateningly on the Thief.)

INN-KEEPER *(Moving between them)* Leave him alone!

STRANGER He stole my gold.

INN-KEEPER He can't have done if he says he didn't. He should know.

STRANGER He's telling lies!

INN-KEEPER I know what you are. You're a trouble-maker. We don't like your sort around here.

STRANGER What?

INN-KEEPER Just because he's a thief doesn't mean you can blame him for everything. Leave him alone. – Go on. Go away.

STRANGER All right. If that's your attitude. I'm going. You're all mad in this country anyway. But don't think you'll get away with it. I'm not a man you can treat this way. My travels have taught me knowledge of strange matters and given me strange powers. Since you've taken my gold, I'll put a curse on it.

THIEF Put a curse on it?

STRANGER That's right. You wanted to learn to lie – well, from now on that gold will make people lie whether they want to or not. Whoever's got that gold will be unable to tell the truth. See how you like that. – Now I'm going back across the mountains to a country where people behave sensibly.

(He goes off.)

INN-KEEPER What an extraordinary fellow! What was he talking about? Telling lies? What on earth did he mean by telling lies?

THIEF I don't know.

INN-KEEPER   Well, it doesn't matter. I've never heard such a fuss about nothing. As though anyone would want to steal a lump of yellow metal! **(He goes off.)**

THIEF   *(Producing gold from under his coat. To audience.)* This must be my lucky day! I was a good thief before, but now that I know how to lie there'll be no stopping me. Telling lies is the most wonderful thing I ever heard of! The possibilities are endless! – And he's cursed the gold so that you can't help but lie. It couldn't be better. I'll be able to lie without even trying!

(Enter Maid-servant.)

I must try it out and see if it works.

MAID-SERVANT   What have you got there?

THIEF   It's a rare breed of fish. *(To audience)* It works!

MAID-SERVANT   A fish?

THIEF   That's right.

MAID-SERVANT   Shouldn't you put it in some water?

THIEF   No, it doesn't like water.

MAID-SERVANT   What a strange fish. It looks just like the stranger's gold. Where did you get it?

THIEF   It was growing on that tree over there. *(To audience)* Very good. I'd never have thought of that on my own. The stranger was right – gold is a wonderful thing.

(Enter Inn-keeper.)

INN-KEEPER   *(To Thief)* Are you still here? What are you hanging about for? You haven't been stealing my beer again, have you?

THIEF   Yes, I have.

INN-KEEPER	What?!
THIEF	*(To audience)* That was stupid. What did I say that for?
INN-KEEPER	You stole my beer?
THIEF	That's right. *(To audience)* I've done it again!
INN-KEEPER	How dare you! Take that! *(He hits him.)*
THIEF	Ow!
INN-KEEPER	And give it back!
THIEF	*(To audience)* Perhaps lying isn't such a good idea as I thought. I'd better stop doing it.
INN-KEEPER	Come on. – Do you want me to hit you again?
THIEF	Yes, I do. *(He hits him.)* Ow! – *(To audience)* I can't seem to stop myself.
MAID-SERVANT	But he hasn't stolen any beer. I've just checked it. There's none missing.
INN-KEEPER	Isn't there?
MAID-SERVANT	Go and see for yourself.
INN-KEEPER	But then why did he say he stole it?
THIEF	I didn't.
INN-KEEPER	Yes, you did! – What's the matter with him?
MAID-SERVANT	He's acting very oddly.
INN-KEEPER	Well, I'd better make sure it's all there. – And you're wanted inside. My wife's getting ready to go to market.

(The Inn-keeper and the Maid-servant go off.)

THIEF	*(To audience)* There's obviously more to lying than I realised. It can get you into trouble if you're not careful. Gold may be wonderful stuff, but it can be

dangerous if you're not used to it. I'd better get rid of it, before I get into any more trouble.

(The Inn-keeper re-enters, followed by his Wife.)

INN-KEEPER   *(To Thief)* She was right. You haven't stolen any. I don't know what you were going on about.

INN-KEEPER'S WIFE   Well, we can't be bothered with him. It's time to go to market. I want you to carry the shopping.

INN-KEEPER   All right. But you needn't think I'm going to buy you a new dress.

INN-KEEPER'S WIFE   I know better than to expect you to buy anything.- Here, take the shopping-bag.

(She gives him a large shopping-bag. Unseen by either, the Thief puts the gold in the bag. The Maid-servant enters just in time to see him do this.)

Now, come along. We don't want to be late.

(The Inn-keeper and his Wife go off.)

MAID-SERVANT   What did you do that for?

THIEF   What?

MAID-SERVANT   You put that fish of yours in his shopping-bag.

THIEF   It isn't a fish. It's the stranger's gold. I had to get rid of it, you see. It makes you tell lies.

MAID-SERVANT   Tell lies?

THIEF   Yes. It's very clever, but I haven't quite got the hang of it yet.

MAID-SERVANT   I know about telling lies. The stranger told me about it. - But why did you put the gold in his bag? What's going to happen when he starts telling lies?

THIEF   That's what I want to find out. - Let's go to the market.

(They go off. Music.)

Scene 2

The market. The music continues while the Merchant and his Wife enter and set up their stall and arrange their goods for sale. There is also a bench somewhere on stage. When they are ready the music stops.

MERCHANT   Well, it looks like a nice day for the market.

MERCHANT'S WIFE   Yes. Let's hope so, anyway.

MERCHANT   We could certainly do with it. Business hasn't been good lately.

MERCHANT'S WIFE   You're telling me!

MERCHANT   Times are bad. And the goods we're trying to sell are even worse. If we don't manage to sell something today I don't know what we're going to do.

MERCHANT'S WIFE   Something will turn up.

MERCHANT   Let's hope so.

(Enter First Housewife.)

MERCHANT'S WIFE   Here comes a customer.

1ST HOUSEWIFE   Good morning.

MERCHANT   Good morning. What can we do for you?

1ST HOUSEWIFE   Have you got any cheese?

MERCHANT   Yes.

1ST HOUSEWIFE   What's it like?

MERCHANT	Well, I couldn't really recommend it.
MERCHANT'S WIFE	It's gone mouldy.
MERCHANT	And it wasn't very nice to start off with.
1ST HOUSEWIFE	I don't think I'll bother then. What's your meat like?
MERCHANT	Horrible.
MERCHANT'S WIFE	It's full of gristle.
MERCHANT	And it tastes nasty. How much do you want?
1ST HOUSEWIFE	I don't think I want any if it's as bad as that. I'll try somewhere else.

(She goes off.)

MERCHANT	Business seems to be going badly again.
MERCHANT'S WIFE	Yes. I don't understand it.
MERCHANT	Do you think there's something wrong with my sales-technique?
MERCHANT'S WIFE	It seems all right to me.

(Enter Inn-keeper and his Wife. The Inn-keeper is still carrying the bag.)

INN-KEEPER'S WIFE	Here we are then. Now the first thing we need is some apples. *(To Merchant)* What are your apples like?
MERCHANT	They vary. Most of them have gone rotten, but some are just covered in bruises.
INN-KEEPER'S WIFE	Oh. I don't think we want any then.
MERCHANT'S WIFE	They've all got maggots in though.

INN-KEEPER'S WIFE	No, we don't want any. *(To Inn-keeper)* Do we?
INN-KEEPER	Yes, we do.
INN-KEEPER'S WIFE	What?
INN-KEEPER	*(To audience)* That's strange. I didn't mean to say that.
MERCHANT	He wants to buy some apples!
MERCHANT'S WIFE	Business is looking up!
INN-KEEPER'S WIFE	What are you talking about? We don't want his apples. They're full of maggots.
INN-KEEPER	No, they're not.
INN-KEEPER'S WIFE	Of course they are! She just said so!
MERCHANT	How many do you want?
MERCHANT'S WIFE	How do you want to pay for them?
INN-KEEPER'S WIFE	We don't want any!
MERCHANT	He said you did.
INN-KEEPER'S WIFE	Yes, I know he did. But we don't want any all the same.
MERCHANT'S WIFE	I thought it was too good to last.
INN-KEEPER'S WIFE	*(To Inn-keeper)* What's the matter with you? You won't let me buy a new dress, yet you're quite happy to spend our hard-earned cabbages on rotten apples. Are you completely stupid?

INN-KEEPER	Yes, I am.
INN-KEEPER'S WIFE	What?
MERCHANT'S WIFE	That would explain why he wanted to buy our apples.
INN-KEEPER'S WIFE	He's just doing it to annoy me. It must be because I asked him if I could have a new dress. It's not much to expect, after all. But he never thinks of anyone but himself.
MERCHANT'S WIFE	They're all the same.
INN-KEEPER'S WIFE	All I want is a new dress. But do you think he'll buy me one?
INN-KEEPER	Of course you can have a new dress.
INN-KEEPER'S WIFE	What?
INN-KEEPER	*(To audience)* What am I saying?!
INN-KEEPER'S WIFE	I *can* have one? Really? Do you mean it?
INN-KEEPER	Of course I do.
INN-KEEPER'S WIFE	Oh, well, that's different then. I'll go and buy one at once.
INN-KEEPER	*(To audience)* What's the matter with me?
INN-KEEPER'S WIFE	I knew you'd agree in the end. – And I know just where to get the one I want.
	(She goes off.)
INN-KEEPER	*(To audience)* This is terrible! Everything I try to say comes out all wrong. I must have caught some strange disease. Or perhaps I'm going mad! I must sit down and rest. *(He sits on the bench.)*

MERCHANT'S WIFE	Well, that was nice of him, wasn't it? Letting his wife have a new dress.
MERCHANT	We didn't manage to sell them anything, though.

(Enter Maid-servant and Thief.)

THIEF	*(Pointing to the Inn-keeper)* Here he is!
MAID-SERVANT	At last. We've found him.
THIEF	*(To Merchant and his Wife)* Has he been telling lies?
MERCHANT	Telling lies?
MERCHANT'S WIFE	What's that?
MAID-SERVANT	It's saying something that isn't true. Like deliberately making a mistake.
THIEF	He's got the stranger's gold in his bag, you see. It makes you tell lies.
INN-KEEPER	*(To audience)* The stranger's gold! *(He looks in the bag and finds the gold.)* So that's what it is! This must be what the stranger meant by telling lies! It's the gold that's doing it!
MERCHANT	Well, I thought he was acting a bit oddly.
MERCHANT'S WIFE	He wanted to buy some of our apples.
INN-KEEPER	*(To audience)* I'm not mad, after all! I'm just telling lies! - I must get rid of this gold before I do it again. Telling lies is terrible. It does nothing but cause trouble.
MERCHANT	*(To Inn-keeper)* What's that you're saying about telling lies?
INN-KEEPER	I said, telling lies is wonderful. It solves all your problems.

MERCHANT   Is that so? Let me have a look at that gold.

(He takes the gold from the Inn-keeper.)

INN-KEEPER   Ah! Thank heaven for that! I can tell the truth again. - Where's my wife? Which way did she go?

MERCHANT'S   *(Pointing)* That way.
WIFE

INN-KEEPER   I must find her. I've got to stop her buying a new dress!

(He hurries off.)

MERCHANT'S   Let me get this straight. This gold makes you tell
WIFE   lies, does it?

THIEF   That's right.

MERCHANT'S   Well, if telling lies solves all your problems, like he
WIFE   says, it must be very useful.

MAID-SERVANT   No, I don't think so. So far as I can see, lying just gets people into trouble.

(Enter First and Second Housewives.)

MERCHANT'S   Here come some customers. - Good morning.
WIFE

2ND   Good morning. I wanted to buy some cheese.
HOUSEWIFE

1ST   You're wasting your time there. I've already asked
HOUSEWIFE   them. Their cheese isn't worth buying.

MERCHANT'S   Yes, I'm afraid that's true. It isn't very nice today.
WIFE   *(To Merchant)* Is it?

MERCHANT   It's the most delicious cheese in the whole world.

1ST   What?
HOUSEWIFE

MERCHANT'S   No, it isn't. Don't you remember - ?
WIFE

MERCHANT	It's the finest cheese you ever tasted in your life!
2ND HOUSEWIFE	Oh, well, in that case I'll have some then.
MERCHANT'S WIFE	We've made a sale!
1ST HOUSEWIFE	How come your cheese is so good all of a sudden?
2ND HOUSEWIFE	What else have you got?
MERCHANT	I've got firm, crisp apples at the very peak of ripeness! Tender, juicy cuts of meat that'll make your mouth water! Glorious, hand-picked, dew-fresh strawberries full of the goodness of natural sunshine!
2ND HOUSEWIFE	Then I'll have some of them too!
1ST HOUSEWIFE	Yes, so will I!

(They crowd round the Merchant and his Wife, and buy everything he's got.)

MERCHANT	I've got sausages that make you good-looking and intelligent! Tomatoes that cure all known diseases! Potatoes that make you irresistible to the opposite sex!
2ND HOUSEWIFE	I'll have some of everything!
1ST HOUSEWIFE	Yes, me too!
MERCHANT'S WIFE	This is wonderful! We've never sold so much in our lives.
MAID-SERVANT	But it's not true! He's telling lies!

THIEF | Yes. Clever, isn't it? – I knew it had possibilities.

(Enter Inn-keeper's Wife with a dress.)

INN-KEEPER'S WIFE | There! I've got a new dress. Isn't it lovely? Look.

MERCHANT'S WIFE | You'll be in trouble when your husband finds out.

INN-KEEPER'S WIFE | No, it's all right. He said I could have it.

MAID-SERVANT | He was telling lies.

INN-KEEPER'S WIFE | Telling lies?

MAID-SERVANT | There's no time to explain now. But he went to look for you to stop you getting it. He'll be furious.

INN-KEEPER'S WIFE | Will he?

1ST HOUSEWIFE | *(Looking off-stage)* Here he comes now.

2ND HOUSEWIFE | Now you're for it.

INN-KEEPER'S WIFE | What am I going to do?

(The Thief takes the gold from the Merchant and gives it to her.)

THIEF | Here. Hold this.

(Enter Inn-keeper.)

INN-KEEPER | So there you are! How dare you go off and buy a new dress? I told you quite distinctly that you couldn't have one, and then, just because I happened to tell a few lies, you went straight off and bought one. Well, I'll teach you to disobey me –

INN-KEEPER'S WIFE	But this isn't a new dress. It's a coat for you.
INN-KEEPER	Eh?
1ST HOUSEWIFE	Brilliant!
INN-KEEPER	*(Taken aback)* You bought me a new coat? Oh...I'm sorry. Thank you very much.
2ND HOUSEWIFE	How *does* she do it?
INN-KEEPER	*(Holding up dress)* But I'm not sure if it will really suit me.
INN-KEEPER'S WIFE	It's the latest fashion.
INN-KEEPER	*(Doubtfully)* Is it? I didn't realise...
INN-KEEPER'S WIFE	Everyone's wearing them like that this year.
INN-KEEPER	Well, if you say so...
	(He moves a little away, puzzling over the dress.)
1ST HOUSEWIFE	Amazing! How does she do it?
2ND HOUSEWIFE	I don't know. But it certainly seems to be the way to get what you want.
THIEF	It's called telling lies. Clever, isn't it?
MERCHANT	It's that gold that makes you do it. It's wonderful stuff.
1ST HOUSEWIFE	I wish I could tell lies.
2ND HOUSEWIFE	Me too.
MERCHANT'S WIFE	Yes, so do I. It's very good for business.

INN-KEEPER	Wait a minute! – Of course! She's got the gold! This isn't a coat at all. She was lying. – *(To his Wife)* Here! This isn't a coat – it's a dress. You lied to me.
INN-KEEPER'S WIFE	No, I didn't.
INN-KEEPER	You're doing it again! – I'll teach you to tell lies.
1ST HOUSEWIFE	Could you teach me please?
MERCHANT'S WIFE	Teach me!
2ND HOUSEWIFE	Teach me!
INN-KEEPER	Give me that gold.
1ST HOUSEWIFE	No, give it to me!
MERCHANT	No, I want it! It's the only way I'll ever sell anything.
INN-KEEPER	*(Grabbing the gold)* Give it here!
MERCHANT	*(Grabbing it from him)* No, I want it!
1ST HOUSEWIFE	*(Grabbing it from him)* Give it to me!
EVERYONE	*(Except Thief and Maid-servant)* Give it to me! Give it to me!

(Everyone, except the Thief and Maid-servant, starts fighting for possession of the gold.)

MAID-SERVANT	What are they doing? Stop them!
THIEF	The stranger was right. Everyone does want gold.
MAID-SERVANT	They're killing each other! Stop them!

THIEF	How can I?
AID-SERVANT	You've got to do something.
THIEF	I wonder what would happen if I tried telling a lie? – *(Loudly)* Hey, everybody! I've got the gold over here!
EVERYONE	*(Except the Thief and Maid-servant)* He's got the gold! Get him!
	(They hurl themselves on the Thief.)
THIEF	Ow! No! – It's not true! I was lying!

(The Maid-servant picks up the gold, which they have left on the ground. A trumpet sounds a fanfare. The King enters, accompanied by the Lord Chancellor, Courtiers, and Guards.)

KING	What's going on? – Citizens! What are you doing?
THIEF	It's the King!
KING	Stop it at once! Behave yourselves. What's going on?
	(They stop fighting, and those that were on the ground pick themselves up.)
	How dare you behave in this disgraceful way in front of your King?
THIEF	It was the gold, you see...
KING	Gold? Never heard of it.
MERCHANT	*(Pointing to Thief)* It was all his fault.
THIEF	Me?!
INN-KEEPER	Yes, that's right. It was the thief. He started it.
THIEF	I didn't! They're lying!
KING	Lying? I don't know what you're talking about. – Guards! Arrest this man.

CAPTAIN OF
GUARDS

Yes, your Majesty.

(The Thief is arrested.)

KING

And the rest of you go home. The market is closed until further notice.

(People start to disperse. The Thief is marched off by the Guards. The Maid-servant waits behind.)

I won't put up with behaviour like this in my kingdom. – Lord Chancellor!

LORD
CHANCELLOR

Yes, your Majesty.

KING

Find out what caused this disturbance, and then come and report back to me. I shall hold a full meeting of the Council tomorrow to decide how to deal with it.

LORD
CHANCELLOR

Yes, your Majesty.

(They go off. The Maid-servant is left alone, holding the gold.)

MAID-SERVANT

But... What about the gold?

(She shakes her head and goes off. Music.)

Scene 3

The palace. The music continues while the scene is changed to the palace. There are thrones for the King, Queen, and Prince, and chairs or benches for the rest of the court, arranged in a semi-circle.

(Enter King, Queen, Prince, Lord Chancellor, and Courtiers in solemn procession. They sit down. The music stops.)

KING   I declare this meeting of the Council open. – Lord Chancellor, what have you found out?

LORD CHANCELLOR   Well, your Majesty, the cause of the trouble appears to be something called gold.

QUEEN   Gold? What's that?

PRINCE   I don't understand.

KING   The Prince doesn't understand, Lord Chancellor. You must explain what you mean more clearly. What is gold?

LORD CHANCELLOR   It's a sort of yellow metal, your Majesty. For some reason everyone suddenly wants to get hold of it. Nobody took any notice of it before, but now everyone's grabbing every bit they can find.

KING   Why? What's so special about it?

LORD CHANCELLOR   I'm not entirely sure. But everybody wants it all the same. Ever since that disturbance in the market yesterday people have been arguing about it and fighting over it and stealing it from one another. I don't understand it.

KING   If everyone wants it so badly it must be very valuable indeed. I must get some.

LORD CHANCELLOR   I did manage to obtain one piece to show you.

KING   Let me see.

LORD CHANCELLOR   *(Producing a lump of gold)* I had great difficulty getting it. The old man I took it off tried to hit me with his crutch.

KING   *(Examining gold)* So this is what all the fuss is about.

QUEEN   It doesn't look very interesting.

KING   No.

PRINCE   I don't understand.

KING   The Prince doesn't understand, Lord Chancellor. Why should anybody want this?

LORD CHANCELLOR   Perhaps we could ask that thief we arrested yesterday. He must know something about it.

KING   An excellent idea! Bring him in.

LORD CHANCELLOR   *(Calling off)* Guards! Bring in the prisoner.

(The Thief is marched in by the Guards.)

KING   Now then. I want to know why everybody wants gold. What's so special about it? What miraculous power does gold possess to make everyone want it so much?

THIEF   It makes you tell lies.

KING   Tell lies? What's that?

QUEEN   I've never heard of telling lies.

THIEF   It's saying something that isn't true.

PRINCE   I don't understand.

THIEF   Perhaps I could give you a demonstration.

KING   Yes, if you like. Go ahead.

THIEF   Could I have the assistance of one of your courtiers?

KING   I suppose so. *(To a Courtier)* You there.

COURTIER   Who me?

THIEF   I'd like you to tell us your opinion of the King and Queen.

COURTIER   What now?

THIEF   Yes.

COURTIER	Do I have to?
LORD CHANCELLOR	What's the matter?
COURTIER	You know what happened to the last person who did that.
KING	Stop wasting time.
COURTIER	Well, if I must... In my opinion, the King is an extremely stupid man who isn't fit to rule over a dung-heap. The Queen, on the other hand, is slightly less stupid than he is, though she makes up for it by being twice as ugly.
QUEEN	How dare you?!
KING	Treason!
COURTIER	Well, he asked me...
KING	Guards! Take this man away and hang him.
CAPTAIN OF GUARDS	Yes, your Majesty.

(The Courtier is marched out by the Guards.)

THIEF	That, you see, is called telling the truth. Now I'll give you my opinion. Notice the difference. *(He clears his throat.)* In my opinion, the King is a great and glorious ruler, justly famed for his wisdom and virtue, in which he has no equal apart from his gracious and beautiful Queen.
QUEEN	That's more like it.
KING	Yes. Nobody's ever said that about me before.
THIEF	That is called telling a lie.
KING	Wonderful! I'm all in favour of telling lies.
QUEEN	So am I.

LORD CHANCELLOR	It seems to be a very useful accomplishment.
QUEEN	It should certainly help reduce the number of executions.
PRINCE	But I don't understand.
KING	The Prince doesn't understand, Lord Chancellor.
PRINCE	Why is it useful?
KING	Why is it useful, Lord Chancellor?
LORD CHANCELLOR	Well... I couldn't say exactly. But I'm sure it's got possibilities.
THIEF	That's what *I* thought. The possibilities are endless!
KING	How do you mean?
THIEF	Well - for example, when people complain that you govern the country very badly you can tell them that it's all their own fault.
LORD CHANCELLOR	Yes!
KING	Excellent!
THIEF	Or if they say it isn't fair that the King and Queen live in luxury while other people are starving, you can say it's because they don't work hard enough.
KING	Brilliant!
THIEF	Or, when you want to go to war with a neighbouring kingdom, you can tell them you want to live in peace and harmony, and then, when they're not expecting it, launch a surprise attack and defeat them.

KING This could revolutionise the whole art of politics! - Lord Chancellor, why haven't you ever thought of that?

LORD CHANCELLOR Well, you never asked me...

KING This man is a genius!

LORD CHANCELLOR He's only a thief...

KING This is the sort of man I need to advise me. I'm going to appoint him to the Government at once.

LORD CHANCELLOR What? You can't have a thief in the Government!

KING Of course I can. It's often done. - *(To Thief)* How would you like to become Minister of Lies?

THIEF I don't mind.

KING That's settled then.

PRINCE But I don't understand. What is lying?

QUEEN It's perfectly simple, dear. It's saying something that isn't true. When somebody tells a lie it means you can't believe what they say.

PRINCE I can believe anything.

KING Give me that gold, Lord Chancellor. - I want to try telling lies myself. *(The Lord Chancellor gives him the gold.)* This gold is certainly wonderful stuff. No wonder everyone wants it. - But wait a minute! It's not working. I'm not telling lies. What's the matter with this gold you've given me, Lord Chancellor?

LORD CHANCELLOR Perhaps it's broken.

THIEF   No, you see, your Majesty, there's only one piece of gold that actually *makes* you lie. A stranger put a curse on it.

KING   Then that's the gold I want. Where is it?

THIEF   I don't know. Everyone was fighting over it in the market yesterday, but I don't know where it ended up.

KING   What? But I must have it!

THIEF   Sorry.

KING   This is terrible! It could fall into the wrong hands. - Lord Chancellor, we've got to get that gold.

LORD CHANCELLOR   If you ask me, your Majesty, it sounds like a job for the Minister of Lies.

KING   Yes, it does, doesn't it? - *(To Thief)* I want you to get me that gold. I don't care how you do it, but I want it.

THIEF   But, your Majesty -

KING   And make it quick. Otherwise I'll have you put to death.

THIEF   But -

KING   That concludes the business for today. I declare this meeting of the Council closed.

(The King goes off, followed in ceremonial order by the Queen, Prince, Lord Chancellor, and Courtiers.)

THIEF   *(To audience)* Find the gold or he'll put me to death? But how can I find the gold? It could be anywhere. How does he expect me to know? - This is what happens when you tell lies. If only I could think of a lie that would get me out of trouble. What am I going to do?

(Enter Maid-servant.)

MAID-SERVANT	Hello.
THIEF	How did you get here?
MAID-SERVANT	I climbed over the wall and came through the garden. I wanted to make sure you were all right.
THIEF	Listen – you remember the gold everyone was fighting over? You didn't notice what happened to it, did you?
MAID-SERVANT	Yes. I took it.
THIEF	You did?
MAID-SERVANT	Yes.
THIEF	I'm saved! You've saved my life! – Where is it? Let me have it.
MAID-SERVANT	Oh, I haven't got it now. I threw it away.
THIEF	What?
MAID-SERVANT	It's dangerous. It makes you tell lies. I threw it into the sea.
THIEF	You did what?! The King's going to have me put to death if I don't get it for him.
MAID-SERVANT	Sorry...
THIEF	What am I going to do?
MAID-SERVANT	I don't know.
THIEF	Idiot! – Wait a minute! I've had an idea! *(He picks up the gold which the Lord Chancellor has left behind.)* We'll use this gold. We'll tell him this is the gold of lies.
MAID-SERVANT	But that wouldn't be true.

THIEF   *(Giving her the gold)* Listen. All you've got to do is tell the King that this is the gold he wants.

MAID-SERVANT   But it isn't.

THIEF   Yes, I know. But pretend it is.

MAID-SERVANT   No. I couldn't.

THIEF   It's perfectly simple!

MAID-SERVANT   Sorry. I haven't learnt how to do it.

(Enter King, Queen, Prince and Lord Chancellor.)

KING   I'm a bit worried about the Prince, Lord Chancellor. He seems to be having trouble understanding this lying business.

LORD CHANCELLOR   It is, of course, a complicated matter.

QUEEN   He keeps insisting he can believe anything.

PRINCE   I can believe anything.

QUEEN   You see? – You must learn not to believe everything people say, dear. Now people are learning to lie, we've got to be careful.

KING   He's going to be King one day. He's got to learn.

LORD CHANCELLOR   Sooner or later someone's bound to say something he can't believe.

KING   Let's hope so. – We must find that gold. He wouldn't be able to believe someone who'd got that. – *(Noticing the Thief)* Are you still here? Why aren't you out looking for the gold?

THIEF   I've found it.

KING   You've found it?

THIEF   Yes. This maid-servant had it. – Here it is, see?

KING	Splendid! Well done! – **(He examines the gold which the Maid-servant is holding.)** So this is the gold that makes you lie, is it?
THIEF	Yes, that's right. I found it for you.
MAID-SERVANT	But it isn't.
KING	Eh?
THIEF	*(Aside to Maid-servant)* Pretend it is!
MAID-SERVANT	*(To Thief)* I can't do it.
KING	What's going on? Is this the gold or isn't it?
THIEF	Of course it is.
MAID-SERVANT	No, it isn't.
KING	Where is it?
MAID-SERVANT	I haven't got it.
KING	*(To Thief)* What's going on? – Are you trying to cheat me?
THIEF	No, no, of course not –
KING	She says she hasn't got it.
THIEF	*(After a slight pause)* Yes, well, naturally. She would say that, wouldn't she? I mean, if she's got the gold then she'll tell lies and say she hasn't.
MAID-SERVANT	What?
KING	Oh, I see. – She's lying!
THIEF	Of course. That proves she's got the gold.
MAID-SERVANT	But I haven't!
KING	Splendid! Hand it over then.
MAID-SERVANT	But I haven't got it! I did have it, but I threw it away.

KING   Excellent!

QUEEN   As though anyone would throw away the gold of lies!

LORD CHANCELLOR   That's really unbelievable.

PRINCE   I can believe it.

MAID-SERVANT   You don't want it anyway. It's dangerous! It makes people fight and quarrel and hate each other!

KING   Better and better! I've never heard such lying!

MAID-SERVANT   It makes people greedy, and makes them cheat and steal!

KING   Excellent!

QUEEN   *(To Prince)* You see? That's what lying is.

PRINCE   I can believe anything.

KING   It doesn't matter. He'll soon learn. – We've found the gold!

QUEEN   Thanks to this maid-servant here.

KING   We must give her a reward.

LORD CHANCELLOR   What had you in mind?

KING   I know the very thing. She can marry the Prince. That should teach him what lying is.

MAID-SERVANT   What? But I don't want to marry the Prince!

KING   That's right. Of course you do. All maid-servants want to marry princes. It's a well-known fact.

MAID-SERVANT   But I don't! I'm not marrying him. He's boring and ugly and stupid!

PRINCE	Oh, no – I can't believe that!
QUEEN	At last! She's done it!
LORD CHANCELLOR	We must hold the wedding immediately.
MAID-SERVANT	But I don't want to marry him! He's incredibly stupid! He's appallingly dull and tedious! He's got spots!
PRINCE	Ah, *now* I understand what lying is.
KING	Yes, everything has turned out wonderfully! – Give me the gold. *(He takes it from her.)* With this gold, there'll be no end to my power. I'll rule for ever!
QUEEN	It works!
KING	What?
QUEEN	Well, you're lying, aren't you? No-one can rule for ever.
KING	Oh, yes…
MAID-SERVANT	But it's just ordinary gold!
LORD CHANCELLOR	Of course it isn't. It made the King lie, didn't it?
KING	*(Giving the Lord Chancellor the gold)* Lord Chancellor, make sure this gold is kept safe. We mustn't let the people find out I've got it.
THIEF	We'll tell them a lie.
KING	Exactly! – To keep them happy we'll let them keep ordinary gold. Since they all think it's so valuable we can use it to make them do what we want. They can give it to people in exchange for things instead of using cabbages or chickens or what ever. And we must get more of it! We'll go to war with the neighbouring kingdom and take their gold.

THIEF   We'll tell them a lie.

KING   Of course we will. There's no end to the possibilities!

MAID-SERVANT   But that's not the gold of lies! I threw it in the sea!

KING   *(Humouring her)* Yes, yes, of course you did. – Now come along. We must have the wedding at once. And then I must go and lie to the people.

QUEEN   *(To Maid-servant)* Come along, dear.

(All go off, except for the Thief.)

THIEF   *(To audience)* So you see? Everything has turned out for the best. I've been made a Minister of State, and the Maid-servant's going to be a princess. Everyone's happy. And it's all due to the gold of lies. – Though, admittedly, when you look back on it, the whole train of events does seem a bit unlikely. But you can take my word for it. It's all perfectly true.

(He goes off.)

The Blacksmith and the Devil

A tale from Ireland

CHARACTERS

BILLY DAWSON, the blacksmith	THE DEVIL
SAINT BRIDGET	THREE FRIENDS
MRS O'CONNOR, Billy's landlady	AN ANGEL
A NEIGHBOUR	A DEMON

Billy's forge. There is a hammer and anvil, a pair of tongs, an armchair, and other furnishings as desired.

(Enter Billy.)

BILLY Billy Dawson's the name. Blacksmith by trade, though if there's ever been a man who did less work in his life then I've never met him. Of course, such laziness is inherited. My father, and his father before him, were both reckoned to be the idlest men in the county, but everyone admits I've improved on my native gifts by my own efforts. And, as if that wasn't enough, there's none can touch me as a villain and a cheat. In all my life, I've never done an honest deed except with a dishonest intention, and all in all I'm the greatest rogue unhanged and the poorest vagabond unstarved in the whole kingdom.

Which presents a bit of a problem, for just at the moment the kids are bawling and the wife's yelling, and Mrs O'Connor the landlady's beating on the door, and I'll be damned if I can think of a single trick to turn a dishonest penny. I'm in such a case that not even hard, sweated labour could help me any, which is something to be thankful for I suppose. But it must be confessed this is a hard life, and a hard world for a man to make his way in.

(Enter Old Woman. She is Saint Bridget.)

SAINT BRIDGET	Good day to you, honest blacksmith.
BILLY	Honest, you say? You're a stranger in these parts?
SAINT BRIDGET	Yes, a poor, hungry, helpless stranger, travelling the roads this cold weather.
BILLY	Indeed, old woman, I know too well what it is to be cold and hungry, but I fear you'll get no charity here, for I've none left for myself.
SAINT BRIDGET	Then God save you too.
BILLY	Yes, it's a hard life. But still, stay and warm yourself at my fire, for I've nothing else to give you, and you look like you could do with it.
SAINT BRIDGET	Thank you, I will. For it's bitter cold.
BILLY	I'll get a good blaze up for you.

(He does so. Saint Bridget warms herself.)

That should drive the chill from your bones.

SAINT BRIDGET	And so it does. My son, you had not much to give, but still you gave what you could. As a reward you may make three wishes, and whatever you ask for shall be granted.
BILLY	Three wishes? Three, you say? Anything I want?
SAINT BRIDGET	Anything.
BILLY	And here's me thinking I'm down on my luck. Three wishes! – Why, I'll cheat the whole town! I'll swindle the whole county! Three wishes! There'll be no rogue to touch me in the whole kingdom.
SAINT BRIDGET	Think carefully now about what you wish for.
BILLY	Yes, indeed, I'll use all my cunning. First I wish that whoever picks up my hammer will be forced to

work with it till I tell him to put it down. Second, I wish that whoever sits down in my armchair won't be able to get out of it until I say so. And third, to keep all the money I'll be making safe from thieves and villains, I wish that whatever I put in my purse, it'll stay there till I take it out.

SAINT BRIDGET You God-forsaken rascal! Is that all you're going to wish for? – tricks and snares to cheat your fellow men? You selfish heathen, have you no thought for your heavenly salvation?

BILLY Oh, by God, it entirely slipped my mind. D'you think I might have one of the three back, and put in a word about it?

SAINT BRIDGET No, you can't, you rogue! I'm Saint Bridget, and I meant to reward you for your one solitary act of kindness, but now you can take the consequences of your evil wishes. I wash my hands of you.

BILLY I've still got my three wishes though?

SAINT BRIDGET And much good may they do you.

(Saint Bridget goes off.)

BILLY Oh, they will, they will. *(Calling)* Wife! Is Mrs O'Connor still beating on the door? – Let her in. *(To audience)* I'll need my three wishes now, for Mrs O'Connor's a fearsome woman when you owe her money.

(Enter Mrs O'Connor.)

MRS O'CONNOR Now then, Billy Dawson, I want my rent. You owe me seven months and I'm going to get it if I have to beat every penny out of your useless hide.

BILLY *(Backing away)* Now be reasonable, Mrs O'Connor. Can't you have a little patience?

MRS O'CONNOR I want my money and I won't leave till I get it.

BILLY   No, indeed, ma'am. I wouldn't dream of you leaving till you've had a taste of my hospitality. Sit down in my armchair and make yourself comfortable.

MRS O'CONNOR   *(Sitting down)* Don't think you can sweet-talk your way out of this one, Billy. I've had enough promises. I want my money.

BILLY   Now, now. Greed's a deadly sin, you know, and haste trips up its own heels, so they say. Sit there a while and learn a bit of patience.

MRS O'CONNOR   I've had too many lessons in patience from you, Billy.

BILLY   But never such a one as you're getting now.

MRS O'CONNOR   What do you mean?

BILLY   I hope the chair's comfortable.

MRS O'CONNOR   I've known worse, but I didn't come here to try the furniture, but to get my money.

BILLY   Still, we have to be content with what we can get in this world. I've no money for you, but you can sit in that chair till the crack of doom.

MRS O'CONNOR   What are you talking about? I'm not sitting here a minute longer. I want my money and – **(She tries to get up and fails.)** – and if I don't get it – **(She tries and fails again.)** – What's the matter with this chair?

BILLY   Don't you find it comfortable, after all?

MRS O'CONNOR   *(Struggling)* I can't get up! What have you done? The chair's bewitched!

BILLY   If you won't leave without your money, then you'll just have to stay.

MRS O'CONNOR   Let me go, you villain! Release me at once!

BILLY   Now, is that any way to thank me for my hospitality? I can't say it'll be entirely convenient to have you stuck in my armchair for months–

MRS O'CONNOR   Let me go!

BILLY   And I won't pretend I'll be able to offer you much in the way of food and drink–

MRS O'CONNOR   Will you let me go?!

BILLY   But do you hear me complaining?

MRS O'CONNOR   Listen, Billy, this matter of the rent–perhaps we could forget it this once.

BILLY   Why, of course! I already had.

MRS O'CONNOR   All right, you rogue. Now let me go.

BILLY   A little forgetfulness solves a lot of problems. I think we could forget a bit more if we put our minds to it.

MRS O'CONNOR   Now look–

BILLY   Think it over for a few days. You'll find I'm right.

MRS O'CONNOR   All right, Billy. Name your terms.

BILLY   Suppose we forgot not seven months, but seven years…

MRS O'CONNOR   What?!

BILLY   That seems fair. I'm a reasonable man. But if you want to think it over…

MRS O'CONNOR   No, no–I won't argue about it. Just let me out of this cursed chair.

BILLY   Then we'll shake on it. *(They shake hands.)* Now you can get up.

MRS O'CONNOR   *(Standing up)* I've always suspected it and now I know. You're in league with the devil.

BILLY   That's a harsh thing to say.

MRS O'CONNOR   How else could you have got hold of such a fiendish chair? You've sold your soul to the devil, and soon the whole town'll know. I'll have nothing more to do with you.

(Mrs O'Connor goes off.)

BILLY   *(To audience)* And that's how it turned out. - Word got around that I'm in league with Old Nick, and soon there was nobody who'd come within spitting distance of my hammer or my chair, and I'm as poor as I ever was. What good did it do me wishing that whatever I put in my purse would stay there till I took it out, when I haven't a single penny to put in it?

(Enter a neighbour.)

Wait a minute! Here comes somebody now.

NEIGHBOUR   Well, Billy, what mischief are you up to today, eh?

BILLY   Mischief? Me? - I don't know what you mean. You're looking a bit tired, if you don't mind me saying so. Why don't you come and sit in my armchair a minute?

NEIGHBOUR   Not me, Billy. We all know about your chair. And I'm not touching your hammer either. We all know where you got them.

BILLY   Saint Bridget gave them to me for being such a kind and God-fearing fellow.

NEIGHBOUR   A likely story! You sold your soul to the devil for them. But you needn't think you'll cheat us any longer, Billy. We know better.

BILLY   Ah, but I led you a fine dance for a time, though, didn't I? Every one of you - the Justice of the

Peace, and the Constable, and the Mayor – you've all paid for the honour of using my hammer or my chair. I made your purses bleed!

NEIGHBOUR Not any longer, Billy. There's nobody left for you to cheat. You've made your bed, so lie on it.

(Neighbour goes off.)

BILLY *(To audience)* Useless, you see. I'm beginning to think old Saint Bridget was right and I chose my three wishes badly. I should have asked for great wealth straight out, but I dearly love a trick, and a man must make his living with his native wit. Now there's nothing left for it, unless I do what they think I've done already and sell my soul to the devil in earnest. But the old fellow's a wily one, and I'm none too sure how to get in touch with him.

(Enter a gentleman dressed in black. It is the Devil.)

DEVIL Morning, Bill. How's things with you?

BILLY And who the devil might you be?

DEVIL Oh, I go by many names, Billy. Don't you know me? I've stood at your elbow a long time now.

BILLY I can't place your face, but your foot looks familiar. Forgive me mentioning it, but that is a hoof, isn't it?

DEVIL Nicholas Clutie, Esquire, at your service. You were contemplating a little business proposition, I believe?

BILLY Well, now, Mr Clutie –

DEVIL Please – call me Nick.

BILLY Well, then, Nick, I wonder if your business mightn't be a little warm for the likes of me, if you take my meaning.

DEVIL   Surely a bit of honest business never hurt a fellow. It's business makes the world go round, you know, and fills a man's pockets with the clink of gold, and that's a music you've not heard so much of late, I'd say.

BILLY   Oh, I get along, Nick, I get along.

DEVIL   Then I'll be doing the same, Bill, for my hands are pretty full these days, and I've no time to waste on idle chatter.

BILLY   No, but wait a moment. Tell me more about this business proposition.

DEVIL   Well now, it's the way with transactions of this nature that the other party opens negotiations. Unless you freely offer the commodity for sale, the contract's not legally binding.

BILLY   You're very precise on points of law, I see.

DEVIL   I do have an immense number of lawyers in my care down below. Naturally some of it rubs off.

BILLY   Then to business. I admit I find myself a little in need of ready cash, and having nothing else to sell but my humble self –

DEVIL   And that's little enough, God knows, but no matter. If you'll be mine at the end of seven years, I'll put down more money than ever a rogue like you was worth.

BILLY   Done.

DEVIL   *(Producing black book)* Sign here. Blood's customary, but ink will do.

BILLY   *(Signs.)* And now, Nick, I'd be grateful if you'd take yourself off. For one thing you stink abominably of sulphur, and for another I'm none too sure your company's altogether good for my morals. My charitable feelings towards you seem to have completely disappeared.

DEVIL   Ah, you're a man of business now, Billy. We'll meet again in seven years. Now I must be off. – Urgent appointment in Westminster. – Seven years, remember.

(The Devil goes off.)

BILLY   *(To audience)* Seven years. I spent five of them drunk, and the other two cruelly sober. It was a rare sum of money he paid me, but not so much I couldn't spend it before the time was up. But there's none could touch me at spending while it lasted.

(Enter three friends.)

1ST FRIEND   Billy Dawson? An excellent fellow. Salt of the earth.

2ND FRIEND   Keeps a good table.

3RD FRIEND   Always buys you a drink.

1ST FRIEND   I won't hear a word said against him.

BILLY   But when the money was gone...

2ND FRIEND   Dawson? Always was a villain. Owes me a hundred pounds from a bet.

3RD FRIEND   I never liked the man.

1ST FRIEND   I wouldn't be seen dead with him.

(The friends go off.)

BILLY   *(To audience)* There's no rogue so despised as a poor rogue. The friends went with the money, and here I am as poor as I ever was. And now the seven years are up, it's nearly midnight, and it's a warm place I'll find myself in tomorrow. There's not even time to be turning over a new leaf and doing some honest work. Which should be some consolation, but it's not easy to look on the bright side of damnation.

(Enter the Devil.)

DEVIL   So we meet again, Billy. How's things? You're not looking your usual cheerful self, if you don't mind me saying so.

BILLY   I was thinking about work. That always makes me gloomy.

DEVIL   Work? You? It's a bit late to be thinking of that. I doubt if you can remember how.

BILLY   There might be something in that. It's a long time since I tried. I don't think I can even remember which end of the hammer you're supposed to hold. **(He picks up the hammer the wrong way round.)** Is that right?

DEVIL   I've never seen such a pathetic sight. Give it here. I'll show you. **(The Devil takes the hammer.)** - That's the way to hold it, see, so's you can put your back into it. Like this - *(He gives a blow to the anvil with the hammer.)* You see? Like this - *(He continues to hammer.)*

BILLY   Ah, yes. I think I get the idea.

(The Devil continues hammering.)

DEVIL   You know, it's a strange thing, Billy - **(Bang!)** - but I can't quite seem to - **(Bang!)** - stop doing this.

BILLY   No? Now that is strange.

DEVIL   It is. I don't suppose - **(Bang!)** - that you've got anything to do with it -

BILLY   Me, Nick? What a nasty, suspicious mind you have.

DEVIL   Now listen here, you infernal – **(Bang!)** – you villainous – **(Bang!)** – you unprincipled – **(Bang!)** – Release me at once.

BILLY   Sorry, Nick. I'm off for a walk.

(Billy goes off.)

DEVIL   Come back here! – **(Bang!)** – Billy! – **(Bang!)** – Come back!

(The Devil continues to hammer while Billy re-enters and addresses the audience.)

BILLY   I wandered off for a while. Begged a little here and stole a little there. And then, at the end of a month … *(He returns to the Devil.)* Morning, Nick. How's things?

DEVIL   Why, you evil-minded – **(Bang!)** – you God-forsaken – **(Bang!)** – You kind-hearted, generous fellow, Bill. – **(Bang!)** – D'you think you could just see your way –

BILLY   You've a little business proposition in mind?

DEVIL   Be reasonable, Bill. – **(Bang!)** I can't stay here – I'm needed. – **(Bang!)** How are all the thieves and murderers supposed to get along without me? – **(Bang!)** – To say nothing of the Government –

BILLY   They do all right, Nick. So what shall we say? Another seven years?

DEVIL   Whatever you say, Billy. – Just let me go –

BILLY   And the same sum of money as before?

DEVIL   Yes.

BILLY   Very well. You can stop hammering.

(The Devil stops.)

DEVIL   You shameless, vile, abominable sinner! How dare you-?

BILLY   Now then, Nick. We made a bargain, remember.

DEVIL   I'll make you regret this, Bill. In seven years' time, I'll make you regret it.

(Devil goes off. Enter the friends.)

1ST FRIEND   Billy, I hear you're doing all right for yourself these days. Let me be the first to congratulate you.

2ND FRIEND   We all knew you'd bounce back, Bill.

3RD FRIEND   Won't you join us for a drink?

2ND FRIEND   And by the way, that hundred pounds you owe me...

BILLY   You know me, boys. Easy come, easy go. Let's live like kings and send the bill to Billy.

1ST FRIEND   You're a capital fellow, Billy, and I'll fight any man who denies it.

BILLY   *(To audience)* But I got the bill, sure enough. The money was soon gone. *(Friends go off.)* And soon the seven years were gone too. And now it's a bitter reckoning I've got to pay.

(Enter Devil.)

DEVIL   So, Bill Dawson. I've been looking forward to this.

BILLY   Yes, it's come to it at last. Well, Nick, let's get it over with.

DEVIL   Not so fast, Billy. I mean to enjoy this. You're going to roast, Billy, roast. What d'you think of that? Makes you feel a bit uncomfortable, does it?

BILLY   Couldn't we talk of something more cheerful?

DEVIL   Oh, no. I haven't forgotten our last meeting. Revenge is sweet, Billy. I mean to sit down and enjoy it. **(He sits in the armchair.)** You wouldn't believe the things I'm going to do to you. I'll invent tortures no-one's ever dreamed of.

BILLY   Oh? What sort of thing did you have in mind?

DEVIL   Well, let me see now...For a start –

BILLY   Perhaps you could put some tongs like these in the fire...*(He suits his actions to his words.)*

DEVIL   Perhaps I could. You're getting the picture, Billy.

BILLY   And heat them till they're red-hot...

DEVIL   That's the idea...– What are you up to?

BILLY   And then take them out...

DEVIL   *(Struggling)* I can't get up!

BILLY   And clamp them on the end of my nose.

DEVIL   Agh! Billy! What are you doing? Stop it!

BILLY   Well, it seems to me, Nick, that if I'm going to have you stuck in that armchair for years I might as well make use of you. Now don't you think if I stretched your nose and took it right up the chimney, it would make the finest weather-cock in the district?

DEVIL   No! No, I know when I'm beaten. Same terms as before, Billy?

BILLY   Seven years and the cash.

DEVIL   Done.

BILLY   Then you can get up. *(Devil rises and goes off.)* Ah, it takes more than the devil to outwit Billy Dawson. The Prince of Cheats is no match for such a cheat as me.

(Billy goes off. The Devil re-enters.)

DEVIL   That's what you think, Bill. – *(To the audience)* You know what he's going to do now. Spend his money with the same false friends and end up poor as ever. But what am I going to do? I'll tell you. Bide my time. I can have patience when I need it. And I'll be as patient as a saint to catch our Billy. I've got the whole of eternity to play with. Seven years goes like that! *(He snaps his fingers.)* And this time he'll be mine. I'll have him before he even knows I'm here. I'll go for his weakest point. And what's Billy's greatest weakness? – Exactly. I'll transform myself into this gold guinea. *(He places the guinea on the floor.)* Once he picks me up, I'll have him. Watch this.

(Exit Devil, enter Billy.)

BILLY   Not a penny to be got by fair means or foul. A man might as well hang himself and have done with it. This is the most unfriendly, miserable life – *(He sees the guinea.)* Well, I'll be damned! A golden guinea. I'll pick that up and put it in my purse straight away. *(He does so.)* Maybe my luck's on the turn at last.

DEVIL'S VOICE   Ah ha! I've got you now!

BILLY   Who's that?

DEVIL'S VOICE   You're in my power at last!

BILLY   Nick? Is that you? Where are you?

DEVIL'S VOICE   I've got you this time, Billy. All I need do is come out of this purse and…Come out of this purse and…*(Pause.)*

BILLY   You were saying, Nick?

DEVIL'S VOICE   Let me out of this purse, Bill.

BILLY   I'll see if I can break the lock. I'll put it on the anvil and try the hammer on it. *(He does so.)*

DEVIL'S VOICE   Agh! – Billy, Billy, dear friend – Ow! Please – can't we come to terms? – Ow! Ooh!

BILLY   What had you in mind?

DEVIL'S VOICE   Seven years and the cash, Billy? – Ow!

BILLY   Let's say three times the cash, and we forget about the rest of the contract entirely.

DEVIL'S VOICE   What? But that contract's legal – Ooh! – All right, Bill. Whatever you say.

BILLY   Good. Then since we won't meet again I'll express the warmth of my feelings towards you before we part.

(He hammers at the purse for all he is worth. Then he opens the purse and hurls the guinea out into the wings.)

Good bye, Nick. It was a pleasure to do business with you. *(To audience)* Well, I suppose you think I went back to my old ways of high-living and free-spending, but you'd be wrong. Barely six months afterwards I was taken ill and died. So here I am again, cold and penniless, and dead into the bargain. Well, there's only two roads to take now, and I think the upwards one might prove the more comfortable. I'll try here.

(Enter Angel.)

ANGEL   Name?

BILLY   Billy Dawson, sir, – if you could see your way to squeezing me in. I've got friends in residence already. *(Enter St Bridget.)* There she is! Remember me, Saint Bridget? Billy Dawson. I did you a good turn once.

ST BRIDGET   I know you. There's no room here for the likes of you, Billy.

BILLY   But it's so cold out here. Won't you let me in just to warm myself? It's not much to ask.

ST BRIDGET   There's a warm place waiting for you, Billy. That's the place for rogues like you.

(Angel and St Bridget go off.)

BILLY   *(Crossing to other side of the stage)* Well, a man must have a roof over his head, and I'm weary with walking and numb with cold. One place is as good as another, I suppose.

(Enter Demon.)

DEMON   More fuel for the fire, eh! What's your name?

BILLY   Tell your master Billy Dawson's at the gate.

DEMON   Billy Dawson?!

(Enter the Devil, running.)

DEVIL   Don't let him in! Bolt the door! Keep him out for God's sake! My bones still ache from the last time we met. Don't let him in whatever you do.

BILLY   This isn't very friendly, Nick.

DEVIL   Keep away from me! I've had enough of you to last me all eternity. - Lock the door! Don't let him in!

(The Devil and the Demon go off.)

BILLY   *(To audience)* So what can I do? I can't get into heaven and I can't get into hell. So I tramp the long, cold, lonely road between the two of them, back and forth, for ever. When it's your turn to come this way, you'll see me, always wandering the same lonely road. But don't ask me for directions, for the only pleasure I've got left is still to cheat the lot of you, if I can.

The Prince's Bride

A tale from Germany

CHARACTERS

JENNY'S MOTHER	2ND MOTHER
JENNY	3RD MOTHER
QUEEN	4TH MOTHER
LORD CHANCELLOR	1ST AUNT
KING	2ND AUNT
PRINCE	3RD AUNT
HERALD	

(Enter Jenny's mother.)

JENNY'S MOTHER   *(Calling)* Jenny! Jenny! – Where is the girl? I never knew anyone like her for disappearing when you want her. – Jenny!

(Enter Jenny.)

JENNY   Did you call, mother?

JENNY'S MOTHER   Did I call? I've been shouting loud enough to wake the dead. Where have you been?

JENNY   Down at the stream. I went fishing with the boys from the village.

JENNY'S MOTHER   Fishing?! What do you want to go fishing for?

JENNY   To catch fish.

JENNY'S MOTHER   Girls don't go fishing. Look at you. You've got mud all over your dress.

JENNY   It'll wash.

JENNY'S MOTHER	You'll be the death of me. Fishing! Girls don't go fishing. They stay at home and help with the housework.
JENNY	So you don't want this fish I caught?
JENNY'S MOTHER	What? - Give it here. We'll have it for supper. *(She takes the fish.)* Just look at your hair! I don't know how you think you're ever going to get a husband.
JENNY	I suppose some husband will come and get me. If not I'll just do without.
JENNY'S MOTHER	And then where will you end up? You've got to get a husband. More to the point, you've got to get a *rich* husband.
JENNY	I don't see why.
JENNY'S MOTHER	You're pretty enough. If only you'd make a bit of an effort. But men expect more from a wife. Especially rich men. The richer they are the more they expect.
JENNY	They'll have to make do with what they can get.
JENNY'S MOTHER	You'll have to buck your ideas up, my girl. Men aren't interested in a girl who goes fishing. They want a wife who can spin and weave and sew and clean and cook and wash and mend and bring up children.
JENNY	Yes, but-
JENNY'S MOTHER	Then there's managing the household accounts, dealing with tradesmen, nursing anyone who's ill, looking after the poultry, collecting fire-wood, baking bread, making cheese and butter, having babies-
JENNY	Nobody can do all that.

JENNY'S MOTHER	That's what a man expects from a wife. And look at you. You make me ashamed to face the mothers of the other girls.
JENNY	It's too much to expect.
JENNY'S MOTHER	If I had a son I'd certainly expect the girl he married to be everything a wife should be. Any mother would. And mothers know best, you know. You'll have to buck your ideas up. You can start by cooking the supper. Come on.

(Exit Jenny and her mother. Enter the Queen, King, Prince and Lord Chancellor.)

QUEEN	Now then, Lord Chancellor, the King and I want your advice on the subject of the Prince's marriage.
LORD CHANCELLOR	I was not aware the Prince was getting married, your Majesty.
QUEEN	He isn't. That's why we want your advice. None of the girls he meets are at all suitable. I want the girl he marries to be everything a wife should be. Any mother would. After all, she'll be marrying *my* son, my one and only son.
KING	And the heir to the kingdom too, of course.
QUEEN	That goes without saying. Don't interrupt.
KING	Sorry, dear.
QUEEN	Idiot. So, Lord Chancellor, how do we find the ideal wife?
LORD CHANCELLOR	A difficult problem, your Majesty.
QUEEN	Of course it's a difficult problem. If it wasn't a difficult problem I wouldn't be asking you for

advice. Really, do I have to do everything for myself round here?

LORD CHANCELLOR   Well, I believe it's traditional on these occasions to invent some sort of test, and invite all the girls in the kingdom to take part. Then the Prince marries the winner.

KING   What happens to the losers?

LORD CHANCELLOR   Well, according to tradition, they're normally put to death, but of course that's quite optional, and we can merely send them away again.

KING   Unless we happen to take a dislike to any of them.

LORD CHANCELLOR   Quite.

QUEEN   But what sort of test?

LORD CHANCELLOR   Unfortunately tradition is silent on that point.

QUEEN   Then what's the use of that? We've got to know what we're looking for first. What should an ideal wife be like?

LORD CHANCELLOR   What we want, your Majesty, is a woman who possesses all the virtues of her sex.

QUEEN   Oh, very clever. I could have worked that out for myself. What *are* all the virtues of her sex? What *is* an ideal wife? That's the question.

(Pause.)

PRINCE   I'd quite like her to be pretty.

QUEEN   Don't interrupt, dear, we're thinking.

(Pause.)

KING   Perhaps it would be nice if she was quiet and obedient and respectful to her husband.

QUEEN	Well, that's obvious. All women are like that. Really, if you can't say anything sensible, then don't say anything at all.
KING	Sorry, dear.
LORD CHANCELLOR	According to tradition, if my memory serves me correctly, a woman's place is in the home. So I suppose an ideal wife should excel in the homely virtues.
QUEEN	The homely virtues! Of course! – What sort of thing did you have in mind?
LORD CHANCELLOR	Well, she should be able to spin and weave and sew and clean and cook and wash and mend and bring up children.
QUEEN	I see. Then that's settled. Why couldn't you have said that in the first place?
LORD CHANCELLOR	Then there's managing the household accounts, dealing with tradesmen –
QUEEN	Yes, yes, all right, we've got the idea. I'll have a herald issue a proclamation at once. *(To the Prince)* You see – we'll soon find you a perfect wife.
PRINCE	As long as she's pretty.
QUEEN	We know what we're doing, dear. Where's that herald? Come along, come along. Why do I always have to do everything myself?

(The Queen, King, Prince and Lord Chancellor go off. Enter herald.)

HERALD	*(Reading from scroll)* Hear ye, hear ye, hear ye! A proclamation from the Queen to her loyal subjects. Attend.

(A number of subjects have entered, including several mothers with their daughters. Among them is Jenny's mother.)

JENNY'S MOTHER — What's all this about?

HERALD — Let it be known that the Queen is seeking a bride for her only son the Prince. Candidates will be expected to excel in the homely virtues and to be in every respect the ideal wife. In particular they should be able to spin and weave and sew, and a great many other things which it would take far too long to go into now. Those who have the necessary qualifications should apply to the palace in person. By order of the Queen. P.S. She should also be pretty.

(Enter Queen.)

QUEEN — I don't remember that last bit.

HERALD — The Prince thought it should be added, your Majesty.

QUEEN — I suppose it can't do any harm. Go and proclaim it all over the city.

(Exit herald. The Queen stays and listens to the conversation.)

JENNY'S MOTHER — Did you hear that?

2ND MOTHER — A wife for the Prince.

3RD MOTHER — An ideal wife.

4TH MOTHER — Are you going to put your Mary in for it then?

3RD MOTHER — She stands a good chance. She's a great one for spinning and weaving and that.

2ND MOTHER — Your Mary's not a patch on my Alice.

3RD MOTHER — What do you mean? When it comes to housework there's no one can touch my Mary.

2ND MOTHER	My Alice is better at spinning than any girl in the district.
3RD MOTHER	That may be. But for weaving my Mary's unbeatable.
4TH MOTHER	Well, if it comes to that, I'd back my Betty to win at sewing every time. I think she'll be the one to marry the Prince.
2ND MOTHER	*(To Jenny's mother)* What about your Jenny? She's not much of a one for housekeeping if I remember rightly.
3RD MOTHER	Her? She'll never marry the Prince, that's for sure.
JENNY'S MOTHER	My Jenny's prettier than your three put together.
4TH MOTHER	Well, what if she is? It's good housekeeping the Queen wants for her son. That bit about being pretty was just what the Prince put in. It's not important.
2ND MOTHER	And we all know your Jenny can't spin or weave to save her life.
JENNY'S MOTHER	My Jenny can beat any girl at spinning or weaving or whatever you like. Why, it's all I can do to keep her away from a spinning-wheel. I've known her spin five skeins of yarn in a single day.
3RD MOTHER	Five skeins?!
2ND MOTHER	In one day?
4TH MOTHER	It's impossible.
JENNY'S MOTHER	She did it!
2ND MOTHER	Nobody can do that. If you must tell lies, at least tell us lies we can believe.

JENNY'S MOTHER	It's true!
4TH MOTHER	Don't listen to her.
3RD MOTHER	We've no time to waste on such nonsense. We must go to the palace at once.
2ND MOTHER	Yes. Come along, Alice.
3RD MOTHER	Come along, Mary.
4TH MOTHER	Come along, Betty.
	(All go off except for Jenny's mother and the Queen.)
JENNY'S MOTHER	But it's true!
	(The Queen approaches.)
QUEEN	Excuse me, I couldn't help overhearing what you were saying. Can your daughter really spin five skeins in one day?
JENNY'S MOTHER	She's always doing it.
QUEEN	Extraordinary. I've never heard of such spinning in my life. *(Calling)* Herald! You can stop the proclamation. We've found the one we want. *(To Jenny's mother)* I am the Queen, and I want your daughter to marry the Prince.
JENNY'S MOTHER	My Jenny?
QUEEN	That's right.
JENNY'S MOTHER	Marry the Prince?
QUEEN	If she can spin like that. – She'll save us a fortune on maid-servants!
JENNY'S MOTHER	*(Trying out the sound of it)* Princess Jenny...

QUEEN	Yes...It doesn't sound quite right, does it? Still, it won't matter. Everyone will just call her the Prince's wife. Bring her to the palace in half an hour.

(Exit Queen.)

JENNY'S MOTHER	*(Calling)* Jenny! Jenny! – Where is she? – Jenny! Come here!

(Enter Jenny.)

JENNY	Sorry, I was playing football.
JENNY'S MOTHER	You're going to marry the Prince! – Where's your best frock? Quickly, go and wash your face!
JENNY	Marry the Prince?
JENNY'S MOTHER	Just look at your hair! You'll be the death of me.
JENNY	Why should the Prince want to marry me?
JENNY'S MOTHER	Because, luckily for you, you've got a mother to speak up for you, that's why. I told the Queen that you can spin five skeins of yarn in a day.
JENNY	You did what?
JENNY'S MOTHER	Now come along, hurry up. We've got to do something about your hair.
JENNY	I can't spin at all!
JENNY'S MOTHER	Well, now's your chance to learn. I've nagged you about it often enough.
JENNY	Nobody can spin that much!
JENNY'S MOTHER	I don't know. You'll be the death of me. I tell you you're going to marry the Prince and all you do is complain about it. Come along. We've got to get you to the palace.

(Jenny and her mother go off. The King and Lord Chancellor enter.)

KING   The Queen says she's found some girl who can spin five skeins of yarn in a day.

LORD CHANCELLOR   A remarkable feat!

KING   Is it? I don't know much about spinning.

LORD CHANCELLOR   Well, no, nor do I actually. It's a matter for women to concern themselves with. We men have to concentrate on running the country. But I assume from all the fuss made about it that it must be a remarkable feat.

KING   I suppose so. And that makes her the ideal wife for the Prince, does it?

LORD CHANCELLOR   According to tradition.

KING   Well, I suppose if we don't like her we can always have her put to death.

LORD CHANCELLOR   Exactly.

(Enter Queen and Jenny.)

QUEEN   Well, here she is. Our future daughter-in-law.

JENNY   Hello.

KING   *(Considering her)* Hmmn. What does the Prince think of her?

QUEEN   He hasn't met her yet. First things first. We must put her to the test.

LORD CHANCELLOR   Quite.

JENNY   Test?

QUEEN Didn't I mention the test? Nothing to worry about. You've just got to spin five skeins of yarn in a single day.

JENNY Yes - look, actually, I've been meaning to talk to you about that. My mother is rather inclined to exaggerate -

KING Otherwise we'll have you put to death.

JENNY What?

QUEEN We've got a spinning-wheel ready for you, and several pounds of flax.

(Servants enter with a spinning-wheel.)

JENNY But -

QUEEN I don't think there's anything else you need, so we'll see you tomorrow. - Come along, you two.

KING Yes, dear.

(Queen, King, Lord Chancellor and servants go off.)

JENNY But wait! I can't spin all that! I can't spin at all. I don't know how. *(Pause. She looks around.)* What am I going to do? *(She goes and examines the spinning-wheel and tries to work out how to use it.)* I don't even know how you're supposed to use one of these things.

(While she is examining it, an ugly, hunchbacked old woman enters behind her. She is the First Aunt. She watches critically.)

1ST AUNT You've got it the wrong way round.

JENNY *(Startled)* Oh!

1ST AUNT What's the matter?

JENNY Nothing. *(She gets a good look at her and is startled again.)* Oh!

1ST AUNT	What do you keep going 'Oh!' for then?
JENNY	It startled me, suddenly seeing you there like that. I wasn't expecting anyone – especially somebody so…somebody so…
1ST AUNT	'Ugly' is the word you're looking for.
JENNY	Oh, no. I didn't mean that at all.
1ST AUNT	Too generous, you think? Hideous perhaps?
JENNY	No, no. I don't think that at all.
1ST AUNT	Then there must be something seriously wrong with your eye-sight. Take it from me, I'm extremely ugly. Always have been. And of course being a hunchback doesn't really improve matters. Still, why should I worry? I'm on the inside looking out. You don't know much about spinning, do you?
JENNY	Nothing at all. And I've got to spin five skeins in a day or else I get put to death.
1ST AUNT	I could teach you to spin if you like.
JENNY	Could you?
1ST AUNT	It wouldn't do you any good though. Nobody in the whole world can spin five skeins of yarn in a day.
JENNY	*(Gloomily)* That's what I thought.
1ST AUNT	Apart from me.
JENNY	You?
1ST AUNT	You want me to prove it?
JENNY	Would you?
1ST AUNT	On one condition.
JENNY	Anything you like.
1ST AUNT	You must always call me your aunt.

JENNY	But you're not my aunt.
1ST AUNT	Well, that depends on what you mean by 'aunt'. If you think an aunt is the sister of your mother or father, as so many people do nowadays, then you're quite right – I'm not your aunt. But if, as is only reasonable, you think an aunt is some kind woman who helps you marry the Prince by doing the spinning for you, then I'm your aunt right enough.
JENNY	All right, auntie.
1ST AUNT	We'll have this done in no time.

(Jenny and the First Aunt go off with the spinning-wheel. Enter the Queen, King and Lord Chancellor.)

QUEEN	Well, she's done it. Five skeins of yarn in a single day. I've never seen spinning like it. She's the wife for my son all right.
KING	But shouldn't an ideal wife be able to do more than just spin?
QUEEN	What had you in mind?
KING	Well, I don't know…
LORD CHANCELLOR	Weaving, your Majesty. That's another thing ideal wives have to do. Spinning and weaving.
QUEEN	Then we'll have another test. *(Calling)* Jenny!

(Enter Jenny)

JENNY	Yes? Did you like the yarn I span?
QUEEN	Very nice. Now we want you to weave it into cloth.

(Servants enter with a loom.)

Here's a loom. You've got until tomorrow.

(The Queen, King, Lord Chancellor and servants go off.)

JENNY   But wait! I don't know how to weave.

(The Second Aunt enters behind her. As well as being ugly she is bent and lop-sided.)

2ND AUNT   Don't know how to weave?

JENNY   *(Turning)* Oh! – Who are you?

2ND AUNT   Fancy not being able to weave.

JENNY   I never learnt. And I've got to weave five skeins of yarn into cloth in a single day.

2ND AUNT   I can do that.

JENNY   In that case you can marry the Prince.

2ND AUNT   No, he wouldn't have me, I'm afraid. I'm not pretty enough. My sister's the pretty one in the family. You met her yesterday – she did your spinning for you. She's twice as pretty as I am. And she's still extremely ugly. The Prince wouldn't have her either. But you – you're pretty enough to marry the Prince.

JENNY   But I can't weave.

2ND AUNT   So between the two of us, we've got everything it takes. We girls must stick together. Will you call me your aunt?

JENNY   Certainly, auntie.

2ND AUNT   Then let's get this weaving done.

(Jenny and the Second Aunt go off with the loom. The Queen, King and Lord Chancellor enter.)

QUEEN   She's done that too. I've never seen such beautiful cloth. She weaves as well as she spins.

KING   But is it enough?

QUEEN   Lord Chancellor?

LORD CHANCELLOR	There's sewing too, your Majesty. And cleaning–
QUEEN	One thing at a time. *(Calling)* Jenny!

(Enter Jenny.)

JENNY	Not again?
QUEEN	You've got to cut up all the cloth you wove, and sew it into shirts.
JENNY	But–
QUEEN	See you tomorrow.

(The Queen, King and Lord Chancellor go off. Jenny stands and sighs. The Third Aunt enters. Equally ugly, she is very short-sighted, and wears thick spectacles. Jenny sees her.)

JENNY	Hello, auntie.
3RD AUNT	You called me aunt! Without even having to be asked!
JENNY	I thought you might like it.
3RD AUNT	People don't often bother, you know. When you're an ugly old maid like me, nobody thinks to be friendly. They don't think you might be lonely, sitting on your own all day, nothing to do except sew – always sewing shirts. And such sewing too. There's nobody sews like me. Have you got any sewing you want done, by any chance?
JENNY	Well, as it happens…
3RD AUNT	I thought you might have. And since you were friendly to a poor old woman and called her your aunt, I'll do it for you. Come on.

(Jenny and the Third Aunt go off. Enter King, Queen and Lord Chancellor.)

QUEEN   She's finished the sewing too. Everyone in the palace can have a new shirt.

KING   Good. I could do with one.

QUEEN   So what's next?

(Enter Prince.)

PRINCE   Mother, I've just met the prettiest girl I ever saw in my life.

QUEEN   Not now dear, we're busy.

PRINCE   But you've got to meet her. I want to marry her.

QUEEN   That's all been taken care of. We've got the ideal wife for you, dear.

PRINCE   But I want to marry this one.

QUEEN   You'll do as you're told. The one we've chosen can spin and weave and sew like nobody's business. It's all settled.

PRINCE   But is she pretty?

QUEEN   I can't say I've really noticed. *(Calling)* Jenny!

(Enter Jenny.)

PRINCE   Oh, that's all right then. It's the same one.

QUEEN   Then in that case we can make arrangements for the wedding.

JENNY   Don't I have any say in the matter?

QUEEN   *(Puzzled)* You? No. Why should you? You're lucky we're letting you off the rest of the tests. Still, if you do everything else half as well as you spin and weave and sew, no one in the palace will ever have to do any housework again.

JENNY   But wait a minute–

QUEEN   So I think we'd better hold the wedding at once. Come on everybody.

(All go off, then immediately re-enter in solemn procession, to the strains of the wedding march, accompanied by the rest of the cast – except the three aunts – while servants set a long table and chairs.)

QUEEN   And now the wedding feast.

(All sit at the table. The Queen immediately stands up again.)

But first I shall make a speech. Ladies and gentlemen, loyal subjects, we are gathered here to celebrate the marriage of my only son, the Prince, to a girl who is an example to all womankind of what a wife should be. Her spinning, weaving and sewing are beyond compare, and I'm sure she'll make a perfect princess, especially since she'll be able to do all the housework in the palace, which means, by the way, that all the maid-servants will lose their jobs. Sorry about that. However –

JENNY   But wait! I can't do all the housework in the palace.

QUEEN   Of course you can, my dear. – She's so modest as well.

(Enter First Aunt.)

KING   Who's that?

QUEEN   What an ugly, hunchbacked old woman! – What do you think you're doing here? Go away.

JENNY   Hello, auntie.

KING,
QUEEN, ⎫ *(Together)* Auntie?!
PRINCE ⎭

JENNY   She's my aunt.

1ST AUNT	That's right.
PRINCE	*(Amazed) She's* your aunt?
JENNY	Of course.
QUEEN	I'm sorry. I didn't realise. You'd better sit down then.
1ST AUNT	*(Sitting)* Thank you.
QUEEN	As I was saying –

(Second Aunt enters.)

KING	Here's another one.
QUEEN	What a hideous creature! – She's all lop-sided.
JENNY	Hello, auntie.
2ND AUNT	Hello, dear.
QUEEN	She's your aunt too?
JENNY	Yes.
QUEEN	Oh. Then you'd better sit down too.

(Second Aunt sits. Third Aunt enters.)

JENNY	Hello, auntie.
3RD AUNT	Hello, dear.
QUEEN	Her as well? – Move up, everybody.

(Third Aunt sits.)

PRINCE	But I don't understand. How can you be my wife's aunts? For she is the prettiest girl in the whole world, and you, if you don't mind me saying so, are the most indescribably loathsome creatures I ever saw in my life.
1ST AUNT	True. But in my youth I was just as beautiful as her. I got as ugly as this by spending all my life

spinning, always hunched over my spinning-wheel, till my back got all bent and I grew as ugly as I am today.

2ND AUNT And I was once beautiful too, but I've spent so much time weaving at my loom my body's grown all lop-sided, and I became as hideous as you see me now.

3RD AUNT And I've spent my whole life sewing, always sewing shirts, till my eyes grew weak, and my body pinched, and I was old and foul.

PRINCE Then it's very lucky I found this out in time. For if people can grow as ugly as this by spinning and weaving and sewing, my wife shall never spin or weave or sew or do any housework in her whole life.

JENNY Is that a promise?

PRINCE I promise.

JENNY Then marrying a prince won't be so bad after all. – *(To Aunts)* I've got you to thank for that, aunts.

1ST AUNT *(To Jenny)* Not at all. Of course, dear, you realise it's not true. We've always been as ugly as this.

QUEEN But wait a minute. What about the homely virtues? She's supposed to be the ideal wife.

PRINCE And so she is. So she can do whatever she wants, not just what you tell her to do. And now that I'm married to her, so can I, mother. – Well, Jenny, what do you want to do?

JENNY Let's go fishing.

QUEEN Fishing?!

PRINCE Why not? Let's go fishing.

JENNY   Are you coming, aunts?

AUNTS   *(Together)* Try and stop us.

PRINCE   Then we'll all go together.

(All go off except the Queen, King and Lord Chancellor.)

QUEEN   Well, that's all very well for her, but someone's got to do the spinning and weaving and such. It just makes more work for the rest of the women.

KING   Fishing...

LORD CHANCELLOR   I haven't been fishing for years...

KING   What are we waiting for then? Come on.

(King and Lord Chancellor go.)

QUEEN   And a lot of help they are! Everyone else is off enjoying themselves, and I'm the one who has to get everything done, as usual. Is it any wonder I get bad-tempered? – Ah, well. I'll go and shout at the maids. **(She goes.)**

Hoichi the Earless

A legend from Japan

CHARACTERS

CHORUS (between three and six)   LADY NII
TRAVELLER   SERVANT
PRIEST   SERVANT'S WIFE
HOICHI   SAMURAI
TOMOMORI   HIGH PRIEST

NOTE: The Chorus's lines may be distributed between groups or individuals as desired. However, for convenience in an unrehearsed reading of the play I suggest that the Chorus is restricted to three voices, and I have numbered the speeches accordingly. In a rehearsed performance, of course, these suggestions need not be adhered to.

The stage is bare. The Chorus is seated at the rear or at the sides.

(Enter Traveller.)

TRAVELLER
    The pearls of dew on the grass fade before noon,
    And, like the sorrows of those now dead,
    Leave no trace of their passing.
I am a traveller. For a long time now I have wanted to go on a journey to the Temple of Amidaji at Shimono-seki. It was near there that the Heiké warriors fought their last battle against the Genji, the great sea-battle of Dan-no-ura. I will go to the Temple of Amidaji to pray for the dead of the Heiké clan.

(He moves across the stage while he and the Chorus describe his journey.)

CHORUS: 1   From the fertile plain of Kinai,
     2   By the shores of Lake Biwa,
     3   He journeys on through the country of Settsu.

TRAVELLER   Autumn has come already to these woods,
     Scattering their leaves upon the stream's foam.

CHORUS: 1   Following the coast road to Western Honshu,
     2   Skirting the mountains where only the pine-trees
     thrive.

TRAVELLER   I wrap a tattered cloak around me
     Against the cold breath of the unfriendly sea.

CHORUS: 3   Passing through many lands,
     1   Past the Island of Miya-jima
     Where the mist swirls like ghosts in the cold
     sunshine,
     2   On to the straits of Shimono-seki.

TRAVELLER   I have travelled so fast that I have arrived already
at the Temple of Amidaji. *(Calling)* Is there anybody
there?

(Enter a Priest.)

PRIEST   Can I help you?

TRAVELLER   I have come to see the site of the Battle of
Dan-no-ura where the Heiké clan was destroyed by
the Genji, and to pray for their departed spirits.

PRIEST   The High Priest of the Temple is away on a journey,
but I know he would want me to welcome you, and
offer you our hospitality.

TRAVELLER   Thank you. Many strange stories are told about this
stretch of coast. Have you heard of them?

PRIEST   Yes, indeed. For many years strange lights were
seen hovering over the sea, and when the wind blew
strong a great noise of shouting like the sound of
battle could be heard. Men say that the ghosts of the
Heiké warriors, unable to rest, haunt the coast.
Sailors fear this place, for spirits are supposed to

rise up out of the sea and sink their ships. Sometimes ghostly armies are seen, bailing out the sea with bottomless dippers, trying to cleanse the waves of blood.

TRAVELLER And I have heard tell of strange crabs, called Heiké crabs, on whose backs human faces can be seen. Some say they are the spirits of drowned Heiké warriors.

PRIEST Yes, they may still be found. But since this Temple was built to pray for the Heiké dead, and monuments and tombs were set up and inscribed with the names of the drowned Emperor and the Heiké lords, the spirits of the dead have rested peacefully.

TRAVELLER I have heard too of a blind man called Hoichi who lives near this place. They say he tells the story of the last battle better than all others.

PRIEST Yes. Hoichi lives here at the Temple. The High Priest heard of his skill in reciting the tale of the Heiké, and since he was poor and blind, he invited him to live here. Would you like to meet him?

TRAVELLER I would.

PRIEST *(Calling)* Hoichi! Come and greet a visitor.

(Enter Hoichi.)

CHORUS *(As Hoichi comes down-stage)*

3 Carefully placing his feet, the blind man approaches

1 Sure of his way without the need of eyes.

HOICHI Welcome, sir. My name is Hoichi.

TRAVELLER I am pleased to meet you. I have heard much of your skill in reciting the tale of the Heiké. Would you recite it for me? I am not rich, but I will pay you what I can.

HOICHI   I'll gladly tell you the story, sir. If you wish to pay, please make a donation to the Temple, or pray yourself for the Heiké dead.

TRAVELLER   I will.

CHORUS: 2   And they knelt and prayed.

(The Traveller, Priest and Hoichi kneel.)

PRIEST   One cry is sufficient for salvation.
O, Amida Buddha, hear our prayer for the fallen
     House of Heiké.
From the endless round of dying and being born
Deliver them, and grant them eternal release,

ALL   *(Including Chorus)* For this life is but a lying dream.

(The Traveller, Priest and Hoichi get up, and regroup for Hoichi's rendition of the story.)

HOICHI   The whole story would take long to tell. I will recite the story of the last battle at Dan-no-ura, for the pity of that part is the most deep.

CHORUS: 3   And the blind man began to recite.

HOICHI   For twenty years the Heiké ruled the land.
They spread over the earth like the branches of a
     great tree,
And in their pride and their prosperity they trod
     down the poor.
But soon the House of Genji rose in war against
     them
And drove them from the Capital.
Carrying the infant Emperor they fled to the
     Western Sea.
Many great battles were fought, many noble
     samurai fell,
Till at last the Heiké were forced back to their fleet.
Of their empire only the seas remained.

CHORUS: 1   Man's glory lasts only a little while,
2   Like a flower that lives only for one day.

HOICHI   Then they came to the bay of Dan-no-ura.
Here they would fight the Genji host at sea,
And, win or lose, this battle would be their last.
The Heiké commander was Tomomori.

(Enter Tomomori.)

CHORUS: 3   Tomomori the valiant, Tomomori the brave,
1   Noblest of warriors, flower of samurai.

HOICHI   He lifted up his voice and roused his clansmen.

TOMOMORI   Men of the House of Heiké,
Today there will be no retreat.
Fight bravely, do not fear death.
For our Emperor, only seven years of age,
Is enthroned upon our flag-ship, under fluttering
   canopies,
The Royal family, the Imperial jewels, the Sacred
   Sword –
All under the protection of the red banner of the
   Heiké.
Never will they fall to the Genji.
Before that every samurai will die.

HOICHI   Now, through the lifting mist of morning, they can
   see
The white flags of the Genji fleet. At least a
   thousand ships
Threaten the Heiké five hundred.
Drawn up in battle-order,
The samurai standing silent on the decks,
The two fleets start to close.

CHORUS: 2   How many of those warriors grimly waiting for the
   fight
Will see the sun go down today?

HOICHI   The archers begin the battle.
Arrows fall like rain, piercing strong armour
Of leather or of iron,
Pain and death falling swiftly from the sky.

CHORUS: 3   And still, among the deadly hail, the warriors wait
in silence.

HOICHI   And watch the distant ranks, spiked with sharp
spears,
Turn into men, then men with faces,
Men whose eyes return their silent gaze,
As enemy stares at enemy.
Then with one voice they shout their fierce war-cry
And the first ships touch
And instantly
Sword and spear flash in the struggle.
The boats lock fast, and men lock too
Arm against arm, sword to sword,
Backwards and forwards over the drifting hulls,
Decks slippery with blood, entrails and limbs
strewn on the water,
Red banners and white mingled, torn by arrows,
Fluttering over the screams.

CHORUS: 1   Deep in the ocean the fish look with wonder
At the descending cloud of blood.

HOICHI   Bitter is the battle, hard the fight,
But slowly the Heiké drive the Genji back.
Above the cries of the dying
Tomomori shouts to his men.

TOMOMORI   See how the cowards of Genji fly
Leaping from boat to boat in their hurry to escape.
Now! Cut them down! Kill all! Let none escape.
And most of all, kill their commander! Kill!

HOICHI   Brave Noritsune hears his words –
Noritsune the lion-hearted, cousin of Tomomori –

And cuts his way across the Genji decks,
Bringing death within a sword's length of their
    chief.
But, as the Genji captain flees, three samurai
Spring at Noritsune.
Parrying their thrusts, he stabs his spear
Deep in the first one's throat, and grabs the other
    two,
Helpless, one under each arm.
For a moment he stands – an enemy in each hand,
Unable to kill them or to let them go.
Then with a laugh he cries:
'Only one way to kill them both!'
And leaps overboard.

CHORUS: 2   And the sea, that favours neither side, drowns all
    three.

3   But now the war god, Bodhisattva Hachiman,
Gazing upon the battle from afar,
Lends the strength of his arm to the House of Genji.

HOICHI   The tide of battle turns.
Those who still live, weary with killing,
Stop to draw breath,
Give ground, and in their turn, fall or flee.

CHORUS: 1   White banners of Genji overcome the red.

HOICHI   Now the Heiké allies, seeing how things stand,
    think:

CHORUS: 2   'This is no fight of mine. Why die with losers
When we can win and live?'

3   And pulling down the Heiké flag, they change their
    allegiance.

HOICHI   The common soldiers and the oarsmen think:

CHORUS: 1   'One master is as good as another. Why should I die
To help these haughty noblemen?'

2   And they turn upon their lords.

(Enter Lady Nii.)

HOICHI   Then Tomomori, seeing all was lost, rowed to the
flag-ship,
Where the little Emperor watched the battle with
seven year old eyes
And the ladies wept.
'How does the battle go?' asked one
And Tomomori said:

TOMOMORI   Prepare! You'll soon be receiving some fine guests.
The noblemen of Genji are paying us a visit,
Therefore let everything be made ready for them.

HOICHI   Then the Lady Nii, who had long made up her mind
What she would do, replied:

LADY NII   Is this a time for joking? Let them come.
But I, though I am but a woman,
Will never fall into our enemy's power.
I will accompany the Emperor, our Sovereign Lord.
Let those who will, follow me.

CHORUS: 3   And picking up the boy in her arms,
She carried him to the side of the ship.

1   The boy looked at her, and asked
'Where are you taking me?'

2   And Lady Nii replied:

LADY NII   Now we must pray to our ancestors and to Amida
Buddha
That we may be admitted to paradise.
Japan is as small as a grain of millet-seed
But now it is a land of misery.
There is another kingdom, where there is no
sorrow.
Beneath the waves the House of Heiké will come
into its kingdom.
In the depths of the sea is our Capital.
It is there I am taking my Sovereign Lord.

CHORUS: 3 And with the child clinging around her neck
She leapt into the sea, and the waves closed over
them.

*(Lady Nii sinks gracefully to the floor and assumes a
pose which conventionally represents death.)*

HOICHI Then, one by one, they followed her,
The strong helping the wounded to the side,
Some hand in hand, some weeping,
Others calm, making sure nothing was forgotten,
All drowned.
Last of all, Tomomori,
Taking the Sacred Sword and the Imperial regalia,
Wearing two suits of armour to weigh him down,
Took one last look at the enemy,
And leapt into the sea.

CHORUS: 1 And the waves closed over the head
Of the last of the House of Heiké.
2 None survived. On the waters
The red Heiké banners were scattered
Like Autumn leaves upon the stream's foam.

HOICHI And of the House of Heiké nothing remained
Except their story.

CHORUS: 3 So Hoichi came to the end of his tale.
1 And all of them, story-teller, traveller, priest,
Were silent in thought.

**(Music. All go off, except the Chorus. Enter Servant
and his Wife. Music stops.)**

SERVANT I am Jiro Kaja, a servant here at the Temple.

WIFE I am Jiro Kaja's wife, also a servant here at the
Temple.

SERVANT We look after everyone who lives here. There's the
High Priest –

WIFE But he's away on a journey at the moment.

SERVANT	And there's three other priests –
WIFE	But they're no trouble.
SERVANT	And then there's Hoichi.
WIFE	But he doesn't count.
SERVANT	He's just like a servant himself.
WIFE	Except he doesn't do anything.
SERVANT	He's blind, and, if you ask me, not quite right in the head. Spends his time telling stories.
WIFE	He was doing it today. A traveller visited the Temple and wanted to hear the story of the last battle.
SERVANT	A visitor? That will mean more work for us.
WIFE	He's the third this week.
SERVANT	What's so wonderful about a blind man telling stories? He doesn't even tell it right. He misses something out.
WIFE	What's that?
SERVANT	There was one of the House of Heiké he doesn't mention. The most important – Munemori, the head of the clan. He was on the flag-ship with the Emperor. Coward that he was, he left the fighting to his brothers. When they were leaping into the sea, *he* didn't push to be at the front of the queue. 'Let's not be hasty,' he said, 'maybe we can come to some arrangement. Perhaps if we were very nice to the Genji they might not kill us.' Till one samurai got so fed up with listening to him, he kicked his backside so hard he went straight into the sea. Even then he swam around in circles for as long as he could, until his armour dragged him down. Why don't the stories ever mention him?

WIFE His mother said he was not of Heiké blood. They'd had a daughter born to them, and since daughters were no use to them, they exchanged her for a boy born at the same time. He was the son of an umbrella merchant, and not a true Heiké samurai at all.

SERVANT So people say. But since she jumped into the sea the moment she'd said it, and everybody who heard her say it jumped into the sea as well, how does anyone know *what* she said?

WIFE I hadn't thought of that.

SERVANT They're all the same, these samurai. You can't trust them.

WIFE Fighting and ordering people about, that's all they're good for.

SERVANT Just because they're born into the nobility they think they can do what they like.

WIFE Rushing about all over the countryside, fighting wars. Burning crops and breaking things.

SERVANT No consideration for others.

WIFE And then when one side wins a war we all have to pay higher taxes to pay for it.

SERVANT And the winning side all get drunk on saki.

WIFE And go around fighting and breaking things.

SERVANT And the losing side all commit suicide.

WIFE At least the Heiké had the decency to drown themselves. Most of them these days insist on committing Hara-Kiri.

SERVANT Typical! If you're stupid enough to think it's honourable to kill yourself, you could at least do it in a civilised fashion. But no – they have to sit down on the floor, slice their guts open with a sword, and watch their insides fall out. Is that any way to behave?

WIFE   And who has to clean it all up afterwards?

SERVANT   Exactly! Not a samurai, that's for sure – If any ordinary person went around behaving like that they'd call him a lunatic, but when a samurai does it, it's noble and honourable.

WIFE   Still, they're brave though. You've got to admit that.

SERVANT   Brave? I'd be as brave as any samurai if I were only given the chance. Why doesn't Hoichi tell stories about me?

WIFE   Where is he anyway?

SERVANT   Who?

WIFE   Hoichi.

SERVANT   Isn't he in his room?

WIFE   No, I thought he was out on the terrace, meditating.

SERVANT   No, he's not there.

WIFE   Then where can he have got to? – It's the middle of the night.

SERVANT   Maybe he's gone into the town.

WIFE   But it's dark.

SERVANT   Makes no difference to him. He's blind.

WIFE   What would he want to go into town for at this time of night?

SERVANT   Maybe he's got a woman down there.

WIFE Hoichi?!

SERVANT What else would he be up to, creeping out of the Temple in the middle of the night?

WIFE He'll be in trouble if the High Priest finds out. – A woman! I wonder what she's like?

SERVANT Well, he won't be bothered what she looks like, will he?

WIFE I wonder if she's blind as well?

(Enter Hoichi.)

SERVANT Here he is! – Where have you been?

HOICHI Nowhere.

SERVANT You must have been somewhere. You haven't been here.

HOICHI I can't tell you.

WIFE You'll get into trouble if the High Priest finds out.

SERVANT Sneaking out in the middle of the night. What have you been up to?

HOICHI Nothing. I can't tell you. I've been sworn to secrecy.

WIFE We know where you've been.

SERVANT What's she like?

WIFE Where does she live?

HOICHI I don't know what you're talking about.

SERVANT All right. Don't tell us then. See if we care.

WIFE We've got better things to think about.

SERVANT We're not interested in what *you* get up to. – It's late. We're going to bed.

(The Servant and his Wife go off.)

HOICHI   I couldn't tell them where I've been. I promised I wouldn't. They wouldn't believe me anyway. I can hardly believe it myself. I was sitting on the terrace, meditating.

(Hoichi sits. Samurai enters behind.)

I heard no foot-steps, but suddenly I heard a voice cry:

SAMURAI   Hoichi!

HOICHI   I knew at once that it was a samurai. His voice was the voice of one used to giving orders. He called again:

SAMURAI   Hoichi!

HOICHI   'Yes,' I answered, 'I am here.' – He must have noticed I was blind, for he spoke more gently.

SAMURAI   Hoichi, I am a samurai belonging to the retinue of a noble lord who is visiting Shimono-seki. He has heard of your great skill in reciting the story of the Battle of Dan-no-ura, and he desires to hear your performance. You are to come with me at once to the palace where the noble assembly is waiting.

HOICHI   *(Rising)* The order of a samurai cannot be disobeyed, so I rose at once and he guided me out of the Temple. *(The Samurai takes Hoichi's arm.)* He did not speak on the way, but I could tell from the clank of metal as he walked that he wore full armour. How far we walked I cannot say, but at last we arrived at a gateway. The Samurai called:

SAMURAI   Open the gate! I have brought Hoichi.

HOICHI   And I heard the guards unbar the gate to let us in. We walked through a courtyard, and I heard feet hurrying and screen-doors sliding open, and the voices of women talking in quiet tones. I could tell from their speech they were ladies-in-waiting at a great court. The Samurai spoke again:

SAMURAI Here I must leave you. You must take off your sandals as a token of respect. This lady will lead you to the noble assembly.

(The Samurai goes off.)

HOICHI A woman's hand guided me along corridors with floors of polished wood, through many great chambers, till we came at last to a vast hall where I could tell a large company was assembled. All around I could hear the rustle of fine silk and the hum of conversation. A woman's voice spoke:

CHORUS: 1 Welcome, Hoichi. We have heard much of your skill. Our noble lord is paying a secret visit to Shimono-seki, and wishes to hear you tell the story of the Heiké.

HOICHI I am yours to command, but the whole story would take long to tell. Which part do you especially desire I should recite?

CHORUS: 1 Tell the story of the last battle of Dan-no-ura, for the pity of that part is the most deep.

HOICHI And I began again the story of the battle.

(Hoichi sits.)

CHORUS: 2 Never before had Hoichi told the story so well.
　　　3 Never before had he been listened to with such attention.

HOICHI I heard whispered comments –

CHORUS: 1 How well he describes the scene.
　　　2 It is as if, though blind, he could see it all before him.
　　　3 As if the battle were being fought all over again.

HOICHI
But when I came to tell of the end of the Heiké, and the death-leap of the Lady Nii with the young Emperor in her arms, complete silence fell over the assembly, until, as I came to the end of my tale, with one voice they uttered a long sigh, as though a sudden cold wind blew through the palace. Then the woman's voice spoke again:

CHORUS: 1
Hoichi, we had not realised anyone could tell the story of Dan-no-ura as well as you have done. Our noble lord wants to bestow a great reward on you. But first he requests that you come twice more to tell the story.

HOICHI
I am yours to command.

CHORUS: 1
The Samurai who brought you tonight will call for you at the same time tomorrow. But I must ask you to say nothing of your visits here. Our lord is travelling in secret and wants no-one to know of his presence.

HOICHI
I promised I would say nothing, and was led home by the same guide who had brought me. – Now I must sleep and prepare myself for tomorrow's visit. I've been most fortunate. This lord must be of very high rank, and will reward me accordingly. It is a great honour for a poor man like me to be praised by such a noble lord.

(Hoichi goes off. Enter Servant and his Wife.)

SERVANT
All day we've been asking Hoichi where he went last night, but he won't tell us anything.

WIFE
It's very strange. He shouldn't go creeping out of the Temple in the middle of the night. It's dangerous.

SERVANT
Dangerous?

WIFE	Who knows what evil creatures may be abroad in the darkness? I'd be frightened.
SERVANT	You're frightened of everything.
WIFE	People say there are ogres and demons about at night. Anyone would be frightened.
SERVANT	I wouldn't. Ogres and demons! They don't exist.
WIFE	They do! And what about ghosts? Everyone knows this stretch of coast is haunted.
SERVANT	It takes more than ghosts to frighten me.

(Enter Hoichi. He crosses the stage without noticing the Servant and his Wife.)

WIFE	Look! There's Hoichi now.
SERVANT	Where's he going?
WIFE	Let's follow him!

(Hoichi goes off.)

SERVANT	He's leaving the Temple!
WIFE	Quick! Let's see where he goes.
SERVANT	Out there? But it's very dark...
WIFE	You're not frightened, are you?
SERVANT	Me? Of course not. But it's very dark out there.
WIFE	Come on. Before we lose sight of him.

(They go off, after Hoichi.)
(Hoichi re-enters, accompanied by the Samurai, and passes across the stage.)

CHORUS: 2	Again Hoichi was led by the Samurai to tell his story,
	Walking quickly together through the silent night.
3	Again they came to the gateway and passed through

> To the vast chamber where the noble assembly was gathered.

(Hoichi and the Samurai go off.)

CHORUS: 1   Again Hoichi began the story of the battle.

(Enter Servant and his Wife.)

SERVANT   Which way did he go?

WIFE   I don't know. It's so dark. And he walked so quickly

SERVANT   How does he manage to go so fast when he's blind? There was nobody with him, was there?

WIFE   I didn't see anyone.

SERVANT   It's starting to rain.

WIFE   There's a storm blowing up.

SERVANT   We'd better go back before we get soaked.

WIFE   Yes. Who cares about Hoichi? Which way is the Temple?

SERVANT   Um...I'm not sure...

WIFE   The storm's getting worse!

SERVANT   Where are we? I'm lost!

WIFE   What are those strange lights over there?

SERVANT   Where?!

WIFE   There!

SERVANT   I don't know.

WIFE   They seem to be coming from the cemetery. And I can hear Hoichi's voice!

SERVANT   It's just the noise of the storm.

WIFE   No, it's Hoichi! Listen! It's coming from the cemetery!

SERVANT   What would Hoichi be doing there?

WIFE   He's reciting the tale of the battle! Listen! – I'm going to see. *(She goes off.)*

SERVANT   Where are you going? – Don't leave me on my own! – Come back! **(He goes off after her.)**

CHORUS: 2   In the middle of the cemetery of Amidaji,
3   In the pouring rain,
1   Sat Hoichi, telling the tale of Dan-no-ura.

(Hoichi enters and sits.)

2   Sitting alone in the darkness,
3   Surrounded by the tombs of the Heiké warriors,
1   Telling the tale of the battle to the stone monument Sacred to the memory of the infant Emperor.

(Enter Servant and his Wife.)

WIFE   Hoichi! Hoichi!

SERVANT   Come back! It's dangerous!

WIFE   Here he is! – Hoichi! Quickly! Come home with us.

HOICHI   What are you doing? How dare you interrupt me in front of this noble assembly?

WIFE   Hoichi, you've been bewitched. There's nobody here. You're sitting in the cemetery in the middle of a storm!

HOICHI   Noble lords and ladies, I apologise for this interruption. Please forgive me –

WIFE   There's nobody there! Only the tombs of the drowned samurai, and strange lights in the air.

SERVANT   It's the fires of the dead! – Come away!

WIFE   Quickly, Hoichi, come home with us!

SERVANT   The lights are surrounding us! The fires of the dead are pursuing us!

WIFE   *(Dragging Hoichi to his feet)* Run, Hoichi, run!

SERVANT   Come on, run! The lights are growing brighter!

WIFE   Run, Hoichi!

SERVANT   Run, run, RUN!

(They run off dragging Hoichi with them. Music. Enter High Priest. Music stops.)

HIGH PRIEST   The world turns like the wheel of an ox-cart, Never at rest. Only within is peace.
I am the High Priest of the Temple of Amidaji at Shimono-seki. I have been away on a journey, but now I am returning to the Temple. *(He crosses the stage while he and the Chorus describe his journey.)*

Turning my back upon the rising sun, I set out on my way,
And, like the sun, travel all day towards the west, my home.

CHORUS: 1   Neither hurrying nor wasting time on the road,
2   Past mountains, woods and streams,
3   Talking with chance companions on the way,
Or striding out alone.

HIGH PRIEST   Now, as I near home, the woods grow more familiar tree by tree. The sun is setting as I arrive at the Temple of Amidaji. *(Calling)* I have returned! Is there nobody to greet me?

(Enter Priest.)

PRIEST   At last you have returned.

HIGH PRIEST   You look worried. Is something wrong? Has something happened in my absence?

PRIEST   It's Hoichi.

HIGH PRIEST   Hoichi? Is he ill?

PRIEST   Worse than that. For two nights now he has left the Temple after dark on his own. Last night the servants followed him and found him sitting in the cemetery, telling the tale of the battle to the Heiké monuments. He's either mad or bewitched.

HIGH PRIEST   Where is he? Call him.

PRIEST   *(Calling)* Hoichi! The High Priest wishes to see you.

(Enter Hoichi.)

HIGH PRIEST   What's the matter, Hoichi? Why have you been going to the cemetery at night?

HOICHI   I have promised not to tell, but since I know you are kind and wise and want only to help, I cannot refuse you. For the last two nights a Samurai has come to call for me to escort me to a great palace where a noble lord and all his court have been pleased to listen to me recite. They have been very kind to me, and have promised to reward me well.

HIGH PRIEST   Oh, Hoichi, your wonderful skill has got you into strange trouble! By now you must know that you haven't been visiting a palace at all, but the tombs of the House of Heiké.

PRIEST   You were found there last night, sitting before the tomb of the drowned Emperor, while the fires of the dead flitted around you.

HIGH PRIEST   The Samurai that called you was no earthly being. The noble assembly for whom you performed were the ghosts of the House of Heiké.

PRIEST   But, since you are blind, you could not know that it was all illusion.

HIGH PRIEST   All except the calling of the dead. The spirits of the dead Heiké are tied to this place by bonds of sorrow and of hate. By once obeying them you have put yourself in their power. If you obey them a third time, they will tear you to pieces.

HOICHI   But what will I do when the Samurai comes to call for me tonight?

HIGH PRIEST   Trust me, Hoichi, No mortal man can save you from the power of the dead, but I know how to protect you. We must write the text of the holy Sutra on your body. No ghost has power against the sacred words. But we must hurry. It's already getting dark.

(During the Chorus's lines, Hoichi kneels and the High Priest and Priest mime writing over his body.)

CHORUS: 1   With their writing-brushes they cover Hoichi with the holy words.

2   From head to toe, even on the palms of his hands And the soles of his feet, they write the sacred characters,

3   Invoking the protection of Amida Buddha.

HIGH PRIEST   Save your poor servant, Hoichi.
Protect him from the malice of the dead.
Let not the power of those whose earthly passions
Still tie them to this world
Prevail upon him, but let the purity of his heart
Bring him to safety in your care.
Now, Hoichi, we must leave you. You must remain absolutely still and silent, and the dead will not harm you. Remember, no matter what happens, you must not utter a word. Now we must go.

(The High Priest and Priest go off.)

CHORUS: 1   Without moving, barely breathing, Hoichi sits, waiting.

2   Unseen by his eyes, the last light fades
And all is silent but the beating of his heart.

3   At last a footstep - a man in armour. Close.

(Enter Samurai. He appears to be unable to see Hoichi.)

SAMURAI   Hoichi!

CHORUS: 1   The blind man sits motionless, holding his breath.

SAMURAI   Hoichi! - That's strange. Where is he?

CHORUS: 2   Protected by the holy words, he is silent, invisible.

SAMURAI   Hoichi! - Why doesn't he answer? - I can't return to my lord without him. I have my orders to carry out. *(He approaches Hoichi, still not seeing him.)* Here is the place where he should be, here is his kneeling-cushion, and yet of Hoichi there is no sign. - But what's this? I can see no sign of Hoichi, yet here are someone's ears!

CHORUS: 3   From head to foot Hoichi is covered with the holy words-
Except his ears! They had forgotten to write on his ears!

SAMURAI   No wonder he didn't answer. He has no mouth to answer with. Nothing is left of him except his ears. - Well, it can't be helped. I must take these ears to my master to show that, as far as possible, his orders have been obeyed.

(The Samurai grasps Hoichi's ears.)

CHORUS: 1   And Hoichi feels his ears gripped by hands of steel.

2   But not a sound he utters, not a single cry,
As his ears are torn from his head.

3   Remembering the High Priest's words,
He prays and suffers the pain in silence.

(The Samurai goes off. Hoichi collapses with his hands to the sides of his head.)

1 Then the footsteps recede, and Hoichi is alone.
2 And the slow hours of night pass quietly by.
3 A little before dawn the High Priest returns.

(Enter High Priest.)

HIGH PRIEST   Hoichi? Are you all right? – What's this? Blood! – Hoichi! Hoichi, what happened?

HOICHI   The Samurai … he took –

HIGH PRIEST   Your ears! We forgot your ears! – It's all my fault. We wrote the sacred text on every inch of your body, but in our haste we forgot your ears! – *(Calling)* Come quickly! Hoichi is hurt!

(The Priest, the Servant and his Wife enter. They tend to Hoichi.)

How foolish I am! – But take heart, Hoichi. A good doctor will soon heal your wounds. And you are safe now. You'll never be troubled by those visitors again. – *(To the others)* Help Hoichi inside and bandage his wounds. – How foolish of me! It is all my fault.

(They go off, helping Hoichi.)

CHORUS: 1   And soon indeed Hoichi's wounds did heal.
2   The story of his strange adventure spread far and wide, and many came to hear him recite.
3   The Temple grew rich and famous, and Hoichi too became a wealthy man, and there were few who had not heard of Hoichi the Earless.

(Hoichi re-enters, wearing some sort of cap or head-dress which covers his ears, followed by the rest of the characters, who form a tableau.)

CHORUS: 1 As for the Heiké ghosts,
          They have troubled no man since.
     2 Perhaps at last they are free
          Of the bonds that tied them to this world.
     3 Perhaps they now rest peacefully
          In their kingdom beneath the waves,
     1 While, in the world above, Hoichi tells their story.

HOICHI   For twenty years the Heiké ruled the land.
          They spread over the earth like the branches of a
             great tree,
          And in their pride and their prosperity they trod
             down the poor.
          But soon the House of Genji rose in war against
             them
          And drove them from the Capital.

CHORUS: 2 Man's glory lasts only a little while,
     3 Like a flower that lives only for one day.

NOTES

These plays are intended to work with a minimum of scenery and props, and may be performed with none at all in the classroom or drama-studio. But they also lend themselves to more elaborate production, and will benefit from imaginative costuming, lighting, mime and movement, and in some cases music. Always, though, the speaking of the words is the important thing, and simplicity should remain the key-note.

My stage-directions are fairly basic, and leave much to the producer's discretion. They may easily be adapted to different circumstances and stages. Casting can also be flexible, and most of the plays offer opportunities for doubling, if large casts are not available. In particular, I would mention that the sex of a character can often be disregarded for casting purposes. Cases where this would be inappropriate are sufficiently obvious.

The Gold of Lies
This story is original.

With its emphasis on event and situation rather than character or dialogue, the play is an ensemble-piece. It should be acted with pace and absolute conviction so that the improbable events seem inevitable.

The Blacksmith and the Devil
This story, and its numerous near and distant relations, is found throughout Europe. This adaptation is based on William Carleton's 'The Three Wishes' in *Folk and Fairy Tales of Ireland* edited by W. B. Yeats (first published 1888; new edition Colin Smythe 1973; Pan Books 1979). I have followed my source with an unusual degree of fidelity, with regard to both plot and characterisation, though I have made a few small alterations, such as changing the sex of the saint, and inventing the character of Mrs O'Connor.

The language of the play is a sort of 'all-purpose dialect' and I have made no attempt to imitate specifically any particular form of speech.

The Prince's Bride
This is a wide-spread story found throughout Europe, but apparently it is of German origin, and appears as 'The Three Spinners' in Grimm (Grimm 14). I have also used the Norwegian version 'The Three Aunts' in *Popular Tales from the Norse* translated by G. W. Dasent (Edmonston and Douglas 1859; Bodley Head 1969). Of course, it shares its central motif with several very well-known tales, such as the

Grimm's 'Rumplestiltskin' or the British 'Tom Tit Tot'. My version - I need hardly say - is very free, and much elaborated from the simple original, not least with regard to characterisation.

Hoichi the Earless

In 1185 the Genji or (more correctly) Minamoto clan completely annihilated the Heiké or Taira clan at the Battle of Dan-no-ura. The story of the war between them is told in the 'Heiké Monogatari', extracts from which - including the description of the final battle - can be found in an *Anthology of Japanese Literature* edited by Donald Keene (Grove Press 1955; Penguin Books 1968). It is retold by Helen and William McAlpine in *Japanese Tales and Legends* (Oxford University Press 1958).

The story of Hoichi is told by Lafcadio Hearn in *Kwaidan* (Houghton Mifflin 1904) reprinted in *Writings from Japan* (Penguin 1984).

The story has also been made into an excellent film, with other ghost stories, by Masaki Kobayashi in his 'Kwaidan' (Ninjin Club/Toho 1964).

The play's form is inspired by that of two Noh plays linked by a comic Kyogen, but I have not attempted more than the most impressionistic imitation. Obviously, the play does not require the elaborate dance and mime of Noh drama, and I have increased the usual number of characters and cut down on the amount of monologue. One or two lines are taken from actual Noh plays, as translated by Arthur Waley.

The narrative passages, especially the description of the battle, may be accompanied by mime and dance and involve extra actors, at the producer's discretion.